Feeding our Families

by

Katie Boyer Newell

To each and every one of you that are in possession of <u>Feeding our Families</u>, thank you so much for helping turn my dream into a reality.

The recipes and information presented in this book have been researched, developed, and written by Katie Newell, founder of Healthnut Foodie. For more of Katie's tasty recipes, tips, and techniques, you are invited to join the Healthnut Foodie community at http://www.healthnutfoodie.com. No part of this book may be reprinted in any form without written permission from the author. For speaking, freelance, or advertising inquiries, please email katie@healthnutfoodie.com.

Cheers to a happier, healthier you!

How I Became a Healthnut
and a Foodie

At the age of four, I was diagnosed with Juvenile Rheumatoid Arthritis. It is an autoimmune disease that causes inflammation and swelling of the joints. I spent my childhood in chronic pain. I had to push myself to accomplish things that were pain-free and easy for my friends. Twenty years later, I was diagnosed with Ankylosing Spondylitis. Ankylosing Spondylitis is an annoying disease that causes the individual vertebrae of the spine to fuse. Eventually, I lost the ability to look up and the majority of the range of motion necessary to turn from side to side. My sacroiliac (hip) joints are also completely fused. I grew up as a dancer and worked in restaurants. Imagine my frustration when I became unable to walk (or even tie my shoelaces) without a great deal of pain and frustration. I vowed to find a way to slow the progression of these debilitating diseases.

In 2004, the same year I was diagnosed with A.S., I had the privilege of marrying my best friend, Darren Newell. Fertility issues are common in people with autoimmune diseases. We knew that we eventually wanted a family so even as newlyweds, we never bothered with birth control. We spent two years attempting all of the "affordable" fertility treatments before deciding to take it to the next level (IVF). When looking at my ovaries, it appeared that I had never in my lifetime ovulated. Fortunately, there were eggs in there, they had just never come out. My hormone levels were also completely out of balance. This was not a good combination. More than one specialist turned us away, advising us to start looking into adoption.

As an active, thin girl in my mid-20's, outwardly, I appeared completely healthy. Why was my body failing me at such a young age? I believed I must be doing something wrong. I began to explore the world of holistic and alternative medicine. I found many amazing books and websites explaining how certain herbs and spices, since ancient times, had been used medicinally to cure disease and other ailments. I was intrigued and studied further. I read testimonies by people who had reduced the effects of chronic disease by nothing more than altering their diet. I read stories of infertile women who became pregnant and had healthy babies. I realized my seemingly healthy diet was full of toxic chemicals, pesticides, and preservatives. I was shocked! My diet was based on whole grains, lean meats, low-fat dairy, and fruits and vegetables. Then, I started reading labels: granola bars made with trans fat, tomato sauce sweetened with high fructose corn syrup, canned soup laced with MSG, BPA, and preservatives. Even worse were foods advertised as "healthy" frozen dinners loaded with all of the same unhealthy ingredients. I continued reading and realized that unless I wanted to spend a ton of money on prepared organic cuisine, my options were pretty limited. I decided I would have to start cooking from scratch. The only (very large) problem was that I didn't even know how to fry an egg. (I'm serious.) I began reading recipes and felt very discouraged. I found healthy and delicious recipes, but most were written for people who were at least somewhat comfortable with cooking. "Brown chicken breast until opaque throughout" isn't exactly helpful to a novice.

Initially, the food I ate was mostly boring and bland, but the more diligent I was about avoiding the toxic chemicals and additives in prepared food, the better my body felt and moved. Darren has a culinary degree and spent years turning me into the foodie I am today. He introduced me to a wide variety of cuisines and encouraged me to explore the world of cooking. We spent our dating years dining at some of the nation's most celebrated restaurants and even honeymooned in Napa Valley. With his help, the Food Network, and lots of studying, I began to learn how to cook. I also learned to use herbs and spices, adding interesting and exotic flavors to dishes without adding fat and calories. As I did this, I realized my body was in even less pain than when I just avoided certain ingredients. Our ancestors were right! Herbs and spices really are medicinal!

Today, I am the mommy of two amazing miracles. After undergoing a converted IVF cycle that our reproductive endocrinologist almost abandoned, she agreed to switch it to an IUI, but we were told not to get our hopes up. However, it was a success! We were blessed with our first daughter, Annabelle (Annie) Grace, born in January 2008. Talk about love at first sight! By the grace of God, and the commitment I had made to my health, I was able not only to get pregnant, but also carry a healthy, beautiful baby to term.

I vowed to raise Annie on healthy, healing, organic foods. I truly believe this will make her a smarter, healthier, more beautiful person. I lovingly made her baby food using only fresh, organic produce. She loved the flavor combinations I created, motivating me even more! I kept studying natural health, refocusing a lot of my time and effort on properly feeding babies and children. I found many studies suggesting that what we feed our babies during the first two to six years of life can give their bodies the foundation to fight off disease in the future, even if they default to poorer food choices later on. As my knowledge grew, so did my commitment to our family's health. As Annie became active, I became even more diligent about the choices I was making for myself. The more I focused on organic, whole foods and eliminated contaminants, the more my symptoms improved. It was crucial to me that I get my body into the best condition possible. I didn't want Annie to grow up thinking her mother was too disabled to play with her!

As Annie grew, I prayed that God would provide her a sibling, either naturally or through adoption. I also prayed that the commitment I made to my health would be rewarded. Imagine our surprise and delight when, just one week before Annie's first birthday, I discovered I was pregnant! Elliana (Ellie) Faith joined our family in August 2009. Our family is complete, and I am so thankful for the way we have been blessed.

In addition to overcoming fertility issues, my body now functions better, and I am in less pain, than ever before. My body's not perfect, but I have come a long way. By choosing live, healing, whole foods over dead, processed, and genetically modified junk, I have been able to dramatically lower the amount of prescribed drugs I have to take. Eventually, I hope to be completely drug free. Because of the changes I've made, my body has relief from a disease that should only be getting worse. I am able to enjoy activities that I thought were forever off limits. Above all, the changes I've made have helped me to bring two healthy girls into the world after being told I had no hope, and I can keep up with a toddler while carrying a baby.

I now believe that food is both a medicine and a gift. Since the creation of life, food has been celebrated throughout the world. It meets one of our most basic needs. Without food, life cannot be sustained. The combination of celebration and sustainability is the foundation of Healthnut Foodie. I create fun, delicious foods that use only pure, wholesome ingredients. I believe foods are seasonal for a reason, so I use what's in season when practical. I explore other cultures and cuisines to learn why different parts of the world eat the way they do. The earth has already provided us with everything we need to survive and flourish; our job is to figure out how to bring it all together.

I am excited to share what I've learned in simple, easily explained ways. Providing our children with a fresh, made-from-scratch dinner is one simple way we can help reduce their overall exposure to dangerous chemicals, additives, and preservatives. It is a small change that can make a huge difference when done in numbers. Please take the next step towards improving the overall health of future generations. Now, let's rediscover cooking the way our grandparents did it.

Real food rocks!

Katie Newell

P.S. – Be sure to check out the ingredients section that follows the recipes! It explains why I chose every ingredient used in this cookbook. As a healthnut and a foodie, I've worked hard to make sure you understand exactly how food heals and why certain ingredients are so important!

Index of Recipes:

Dinners for Spring

Pork Vindaloo

Savory Springtime Napolean

Seared Halibut in a Tomato-Rosemary Broth

Rockfish and Sesame Udon Noodle Bowl

Creamy Cumin-Lime Taco Salad

Fried Egg and Roast Beef Hash

Asparagus and Spaghetti alla Carbonara

Coconut Chicken with German Potato Salad

Leek, Wild Rice and Mushroom Soup

Chicken Marsala over Parsleyed Egg Noodles

Classic Bolognese

Chicken and Mango Thai Salad

Pork Vindaloo

with saffron rice and simple veggies

START TO FINISH: 60 MINUTES, 25 MINUTES ACTIVE

Pork Vindaloo is a traditional dish from the Goa district of India. It involves a long list of toasted and ground spices. When traditionally prepared, pork vindaloo tastes amazing, but is too spicy to be family friendly. Determined to create a seasoning profile mild enough to appeal to kids (while still delivering authentic flavors), we began to play around with the spice combinations. This version is a total success!

For the vindaloo:

1	- 1¼ lb pork tenderloin, cut into 1 inch cubes	1	onion, thinly sliced
1	cup frozen peas	4	garlic cloves, minced
1	cup diced carrots, fresh or frozen	2	tbsp extra virgin olive oil
		1	cup light coconut milk

For the rice:

1	cup brown jasmine rice		Small pinch saffron threads
2	cups chicken broth	¼	cup cilantro, coarsely chopped

For the vindaloo paste:

1½	tsp ground garlic	½	tsp fresh ground black pepper
1	tsp ground coriander		
1	tsp ground cumin	½	tsp organic sugar
1	tsp smoked paprika	¼	tsp cardamon
1	tsp sea salt	¼	tsp ground cayenne
½	tsp ground mustard	¼	tsp cinnamon
½	tsp ground turmeric	¼	cup apple cider vinegar

Pork vindaloo is a great kid-friendly meal that is naturally gluten-free and nut-free. Annie thinks saffron rice is amazing, so I make a double batch for her to munch on throughout the week. Vegetarians can substitute three cups of prepared garbanzo beans (or two cans) for the pork and prepare your rice with vegetable broth instead of chicken broth. This recipe serves four adults and the leftovers reheat fabulously.

Preparations:

Prepare the vindaloo paste: Combine all ingredients listed under "for the vindaloo paste". Set aside.

Slicing and dicing: Thinly slice 1 onion. Mince 4 cloves garlic. If necessary, dice 1 cup carrots.

Cube pork tenderloin: Cut pork tenderloin into 1-inch (bite size) cubes.

Instructions:

Cook the rice: One hour before you wish to eat dinner, bring 2 cups chicken broth and a small pinch of saffron threads just to a boil. Add 1 cup brown jasmine rice. Stir and cover with a tight fitting lid. Reduce heat and simmer according to package directions.

When 25 minutes remains on the rice, start your vindaloo: Heat a large deep skillet over medium heat for about 5 minutes. Add 2 tbsp extra virgin olive oil and heat an additional 30 seconds, until oil shimmers. Sauté onion and garlic for 3 minutes in hot oil. Add vindaloo paste to skillet and stir continuously for 2 - 3 minutes, until the vinegar has mostly evaporated. Place cubed pork into skillet. Allow pork to brown, stirring occasionally, for 3 - 4 minutes. Add coconut milk, frozen peas, and carrots. Stir for about a minute to deglaze pan and to incorporate the spices throughout. Simmer vindaloo for 15 minutes.

Getting it on the table: When vindaloo is almost ready, coarsely chop ¼ cup cilantro, leaves and tender stems only. Fluff saffron rice with a fork, and transfer to serving platter. Pour vindaloo over rice. Garnish with coarsely chopped cilantro. Serve and enjoy!

Quick tip!!! When buying your pork directly from the butcher, ask him to cube your tenderloin for you! He should be more than happy to oblige.

The next time I make this, I want to try..._____

My actual cooking times for this dish were..._____

I'm going to share this recipe with..._____

3

Savory Springtime Napoleon
seasonal produce bound with herbed eggs and potatoes

START TO FINISH: 1 HOUR 20 MINUTES, 20 MINUTES ACTIVE

This is a great, affordable meal that you can feel good about feeding your whole family. Eggs are one of the most economical sources of protein available; they really deserve a chance to shine at dinner as well. This dish was created in an attempt to give quiche a healthy makeover. Thinly sliced potatoes serve as the "crust" and layers of vegetables act as the napoleon. After layering, top the veggies with a seasoned egg mixture, sprinkle with cheese, and pop it in the oven. This dinner (or brunch) is amazing, satisfying, and super budget friendly. You can even make two of these napoleons at a time, popping the second one in the freezer for an upcoming busy night. It is always great to know there is a healthy, easy meal on standby!

For the napoleon:
- 1 pound red potatoes, thinly sliced
- 1 bunch asparagus, trimmed
- 1 beefsteak tomato, thinly sliced
- 1 leek, thinly sliced, white and pale green parts only
- ½ cup shredded Gruyere cheese (or Swiss)
- 1 tbsp extra virgin olive oil

For the egg mixture:
- 4 eggs
- 1½ cups milk (I used organic whole)
- 1 tbsp dry mustard
- 1 tsp smoked paprika
- ½ tsp ground turmeric

To season the potatoes:
- 1 tsp ground coriander
- 1 tsp ground cumin
- 1 tsp sea salt
- ½ tsp white pepper

This springtime napoleon is a great dish, easily adapted to whatever veggies you have on hand. The first time we made this, Darren and I were actually shocked at how well it turned out. Annie and Ellie also really enjoy it and the leftovers taste great reheated. It is naturally vegetarian, gluten-free, and nut-free. Serves four to six.

4

Instructions:

Preparations: In a small bowl or ramekin, combine all ingredients listed under "to season the potatoes". Set aside. In a mixing bowl or 1-quart glass measuring dish, whisk together all ingredients listed under "for the egg mixture". Grate ½ cup Gruyere cheese. Thinly slice 1 leek, white and pale green parts only. The dark green parts of the leek are bitter and should not be eaten. Snap ends off of asparagus. Just before layering, thinly slice 1 pound of red potatoes (about ¼ inch thick, I used a mandolin) and 1 large beefsteak tomato.

Preheat oven to 400 degrees.

While oven heats, prepare your napoleon: Toss the potatoes with 1 tbsp extra virgin olive oil. Arrange half of the potatoes on the bottom of an 8 x 8 inch glass baking dish. Sprinkle about half of the combined seasonings on top of the potatoes. Repeat with remaining potatoes and spices. Cover potatoes with shredded gruyere cheese and about half of the leeks. Layer the tomato slices on top of the leeks. Season tomatoes with ¼ tsp each sea salt and fresh ground black pepper. Lay asparagus in a single layer on top of the tomato. I put all of the flat ends against the sides. The little tops slightly overlapped in the middle, but whatever works for you is fine. Sprinkle remaining leeks over asparagus. Whisk egg mixture one more time to evenly distribute spices and then pour over the entire dish.

Bake dish for 45 – 60 minutes, until egg mixture is set in the center.

> **Quick tip!!!** To get your napoleon slices to look like the one pictured, use a serrated knife (tomato knife) to cut it into squares. If you use a regular serving spoon, the asparagus won't break off as nicely and the beautiful layering will lose its affect.

The next time I make this, I want to try..._____

My actual cooking times for this dish were..._____

I'm going to share this recipe with..._____

Halibut with Beans and Rice
in a simply prepared rosemary infused tomato broth

START TO FINISH: 25 MINUTES, MOSTLY ACTIVE

What great flavors! This is a nutritious and satisfying meal that tastes like something you would order in an upscale restaurant. A few years back, I saw a recipe for rosemary broth in some magazine and was intrigued. We added beans, rice, and tomatoes to make this a complete meal that will wow your whole family. This dinner has little prep and goes start to finish in just 25 minutes. Because fish spoils quicker than other leftovers, this recipe serves just two adults and two small children. If you are a larger family, double or even triple the recipe.

2 halibut fillets, 6 – 8 ounces each	1 sprig fresh rosemary, plus garnish
1½ cups prepared white beans (or one 15-oz can)	½ cup dry white wine
1 cup cooked brown rice	1 tbsp + 2 tsp extra virgin olive oil
1 pint cherry tomatoes	¼ tsp + ½ tsp sea salt
3 cloves garlic	¼ tsp + ½ tsp fresh ground black pepper
1½ cups chicken broth	

> Are you excited?!? You are about to prepare a dish worthy of any fine dining establishment in your very own kitchen. The delicate flavors and textures of this dish make it super kid-friendly. Beans and rice form a complete protein, so vegetarians simply omit the halibut and use vegetable broth in place of chicken broth. This dish is naturally gluten-free and free of any nuts or nut products.

Preparations:

Halve one pint cherry tomatoes.
Peel and mince 3 cloves garlic.
Remove rosemary leaves from thick stems and coarsely chop.
If necessary, drain and rinse white beans.

Instructions:

Cook your halibut: Heat a large flat skillet over medium high heat for about 5 minutes. While skillet heats, season halibut fillets with ¼ tsp each sea salt and fresh ground black pepper. When skillet is hot, add 1 tbsp extra virgin olive oil and heat an additional 30 seconds, until oil shimmers. Place halibut in hot oil and sear for 3 - 5 minutes per side (depending on how thin or thick your fillets are, and whether you prefer your fish more or less done). When flipping the fish, shimmy the pan to allow the extra oil to get under the second side. This is how you obtain the nice brown crust you see in restaurants, and it helps prevent the fish from sticking. When the halibut is cooked to your liking, transfer to cutting board and loosely cover with a foil tent to keep it hot.

> **Quick tip!!!** If your fish sticks when it is time to flip, pour a little more oil under the part of the fillet that you can get loose. Allow the fish to brown for a minute longer and then try flipping again.

Prepare your broth: Place remaining 2 tsp olive oil and minced garlic in the now empty skillet. Sauté for 30 - 45 seconds, stirring up any browned fish bits until skillet is clean (these little guys give a great flavor to the broth). Stir in 1½ cups chicken broth, ½ cup dry white wine, halved cherry tomatoes, beans, rice, and ½ tsp each sea salt and black pepper. Bring mixture just to a boil. Reduce heat to medium low. Stir in chopped rosemary and allow broth to simmer for 6 - 7 minutes (to allow the rosemary to infuse the broth). Turn off heat.

Pulling it all together: Ladle bean, rice, and tomato mixture into shallow bowls. If you are just serving two people, you probably won't need all of the beans and rice. (Don't worry, it makes a great lunch the next day!) Top each bowl with a halibut fillet and garnish with a rosemary sprig, if desired. Serve and enjoy!

The next time I make this, I want to try..._____

My actual cooking times for this dish were..._____

I'm going to share this recipe with..._____

Rockfish and Sesame Udon Noodle Bowl

START TO FINISH: 25 MINUTES, MOSTLY INACTIVE

This dish was inspired after our family ate at an Asian food court in Los Angeles. We were served piping hot bowls of fresh ramen in a rich pork broth that was garnished with scallions. A few days before that, I read about a technique to steam fish over the soup you intend to serve it with. Combining the two dishes seemed like a match made in heaven. It took quite a few attempts to get everything just perfect, but this meal is now one of our family's favorite dinners. White flaky fish swimming in a savory and vegetable packed broth was something that even Ellie was able to enjoy at a very young age. Again, because fish quickly spoils (and the udon noodles expand and get gummy), this recipe provides just enough for our small family (two adults and two small children). If you are a larger family or are entertaining friends, double or triple this recipe.

½	pound rockfish, or any white flaky fish	5	cups chicken broth
1	square-inch (3 ounces) dried udon noodles	2	tsp corn starch
		2	tbsp filtered water
8	oz can water chestnuts	1	tbsp sesame oil
1	cup frozen corn kernels	1	tbsp soy sauce
1	cup frozen peas	⅛	tsp cayenne pepper
1	cup sliced mushrooms	½	tsp sea salt
1	inch piece fresh ginger	½	tsp fresh ground black pepper
⅓	cup dry sherry		Sriracha hot sauce, if desired
2	green onions		

I often make this dinner on nights when Darren will get home right at dinnertime. The super easy prep and clean up allows us to spend our precious family time playing, not cleaning up the kitchen! Vegetarians can use extra firm tofu in place of the fish, omitting the steaming process, adding the ginger with the other veggies, and replacing the chicken broth with vegetable broth. Those sensitive to gluten can substitute 100% buckwheat soba noodles in place of the udon noodles. This dish is naturally free of any nuts or nut products.

Instructions:

Prepare your ingredients: Trim and thinly slice 2 scallions. Peel and coarsely chop a 1-inch piece of ginger. Press ginger through garlic press (or mince with a knife). Season rockfish with ½ tsp each sea salt and fresh ground black pepper. Rub ginger on top of fish fillets.

Steam your fish and simmer your vegetables: Bring 5 cups of chicken broth just to a boil over medium high heat. Place ginger rubbed rockfish in steamer insert and steam (covered) for about 8 minutes. Remove fish and steamer insert and set aside. Add 1 cup each frozen corn, peas, and sliced mushrooms to broth. Return broth just to a boil. Reduce heat to medium and add ⅓ cup dry sherry, 1 tbsp each soy sauce and sesame oil, and ⅛ tsp cayenne. Simmer uncovered for 10 minutes.

> **No special steamer? No problem!** If you do not have a pot with a raised steamer insert, you can bake your ginger rubbed fish in a 350 degree oven for 15 minutes while you prepare the soup. Otherwise, proceed as written!

Finishing your dish: When 10 minutes have lapsed, flake fish into pot. Add dried udon noodles and water chestnuts to soup. Increase heat back to medium high and boil noodles for 4 minutes (or according to package directions). While noodles cook, dissolve 2 tsp cornstarch into 2 tbsp water. Add cornstarch paste and stir continuously a minute more to thicken broth. Turn off heat. Ladle soup into bowls and garnish with sliced green onions. If desired, pass Sriracha at the table. Serve immediately and enjoy!

> **Quick tip!!!** When purchasing fish, any white flaky fish will do. Tell your fishmonger that you want a flaky white fish that is fresh, sustainably raised, and on sale. He can help guide you from there. To save a few pennies, you can also buy your fish frozen. Because it is frozen immediately after being cleaned, frozen fish is often even fresher than what you would find in the display case!

The next time I make this, I want to try..._____

My actual cooking times for this dish were..._____

I'm going to share this recipe with..._____

Creamy Cumin-Lime Taco Salad

START TO FINISH: 20 MINUTES, MOSTLY ACTIVE

"This is a winner!" That is what Darren said the first time he devoured this salad. Turning it upside down and using crunchy romaine lettuce as the base (instead of chips) saves you hundreds of nutrient sparse calories. Making your own taco seasoning is super easy, reduces your exposure to preservatives, and is much more cost effective than buying the mix. Because leftover salad rarely gets eaten, I have written this recipe to feed just two to three adults (or two adults and two small children). If you have a larger family (or want leftovers), double or even triple the recipe. (Store dressing and salad separately.)

For the salad:

6	cups romaine lettuce (one 9-ounce bag)	½	cup Monterrey Jack cheese, shredded
1	cup cherry tomatoes	½	cup cilantro
½	cup red onion	½	cup crushed organic tortilla chips
½	cup frozen corn kernels	1	tsp extra virgin olive oil
½	pound grass-fed ground beef		

For the dressing:

2	tbsp prepared salsa	¼	tsp chili powder
2	tbsp sour cream	¼	tsp sea salt
2	tsp mayonnaise	¼	tsp freshly ground black pepper
½	tsp ground cumin	1	wedge of lime
¼	tsp dried basil		

For the taco seasoning:

2	tbsp ground cumin	½	tsp sea salt
1	tsp garlic powder	½	tsp freshly ground black pepper
½	tsp chili powder		
¼	tsp organic sugar		

This is a simple, delicious, and nutritious dinner. Vegetarians can enjoy this dish as written using non-GMO soy crumbles in place of the ground beef. When used with organic corn tortilla chips (double check the ingredients), this dish is naturally gluten-free and nut-free.

Instructions:

Prepare the creamy cumin-lime salad dressing: Whisk together all ingredients listed under "for the dressing".

Prepare your taco seasonings: In a small bowl or ramekin, combine all ingredients listed under "for the taco seasoning.

> **Work ahead!** You can speed up dinner even more by preparing the dressing and the taco seasoning up to three days in advance.

Prep your produce: Dice ½ cup red onion (½ small, ¼ large), Coarsely chop ½ cup cilantro (leaves and tender stems only) and 6 cups romaine lettuce. Halve cherry tomatoes.

Brown your beef: Heat a medium or large skillet over medium high heat for about 5 minutes. Add 1 tsp extra virgin olive oil and heat an additional 30 seconds, until oil shimmers. Set aside 1 tbsp diced red onion for garnish. Add remaining onion and corn kernels to skillet. Sauté for about 1 minute, just to allow onions to "sweat". Add ground beef and combined seasonings. Brown beef, corn, onion, and spices for about 5 minutes, until beef is no longer pink. Turn off heat.

Getting it on the table: Toss chopped romaine and cilantro with creamy cumin-lime dressing. Divide equally among plates. To each plate, add some of the meat mixture, halved cherry tomatoes, and shredded Monterey jack cheese. Garnish with a sprinkling of crushed tortilla chips and reserved red onion.

> **Quick tips!!!** Browning your ground beef with corn and onion is a great way to bulk up your dish without bulking up your body! It is also a great way to stretch your food dollar and make everyone feel as though they are getting a larger portion of meat. If your toddler is anti-lettuce like mine, try serving the remaining components of the salad on a bed of diced avocado instead.

The next time I make this, I am going to try..._____

My actual cooking times for this dish were..._____

I'm going to share this recipe with..._____

Fried Egg and Roast Beef Hash
served alongside mixed greens in a tarragon vinaigrette

START TO FINISH: 35 MINUTES. 20 MINUTES ACTIVE

Hash, comfort food at its finest, is an inexpensive, quick, and easy meal that is great for busy nights. We like to make this with leftover St. Patrick's Day corned beef or pot roast. No leftovers on hand? No problem! Just pick up a pound of thick-cut roast beef from the deli counter (nitrate-free, of course). Potatoes have a bad reputation, mostly because they are usually fried in unhealthy oils or mashed with loads of cream and butter. You will be pleasantly surprised to learn that the humble spud contains almost as many healing antioxidants and phytonutrients as broccoli! Be sure to leave the skin on to retain all of these great nutrients. Our "healthified" version of this popular comfort food is sure to please your whole family!

For the hash:

2	medium baking potatoes, about a pound	1	tsp sea salt
3	cups roast beef, cubed	¾	tsp fresh ground black pepper
1	large red onion	½	tbsp butter
2	cloves garlic	1	egg per person
1	cup chicken broth		Fresh parsley, to garnish
1	tsp dried thyme		

For the mixed greens and tarragon vinaigrette:

3	tbsp extra virgin olive oil	½	tsp freshly ground black pepper
1	tbsp red wine vinegar	4	to 5 cups mixed greens (5-oz bag)
½	tsp dried tarragon		
¼	tsp organic sugar		
½	tsp sea salt		

Annie and Ellie gobble up every part of this meal (except they have fruit instead of greens). This roast beef hash also makes a great brunch dish and is the perfect thing to serve at a late morning playdate. It is naturally gluten-free and nut-free. Vegetarians can use chopped mushrooms in place of the beef and vegetable broth in place of chicken broth. Serves four to six, leftovers taste great!

Preparations:

Slicing and dicing: Dice 1 onion and 2 cloves garlic. Cube 2 baking potatoes and 3 cups leftover beef. (Shredded beef also works.)

Prepare your vinaigrette: Aside from the mixed greens, whisk together all ingredients listed under "for the mixed greens and tarragon vinaigrette". (The vinaigrette can be made up to 3 days ahead.)

Instructions:

Prepare your hash: Heat a large deep skillet over medium high heat for about 5 minutes. When the skillet is hot, add 2 tbsp extra virgin olive oil and heat an additional 30 seconds, until oil shimmers. Add onion and garlic to skillet and sauté for about 5 minutes. Add potatoes, ¼ cup chicken broth, 1 tsp dried thyme, 1 tsp sea salt, and ¾ tsp freshly ground black pepper to skillet. Sauté for 3 minutes more. Pour remaining chicken broth over mixture. Cover with a tight fitting lid, reduce heat to medium, and simmer for 15 minutes or until potatoes are tender. Remove lid and add chopped beef. Sauté until the beef is hot and most of the liquid has been absorbed, about 5 minutes. Transfer to your serving platter.

Fry your eggs: Place ½ tbsp butter in the now empty skillet. When butter is melted, crack eggs into skillet and fry for about 2 minutes per side. Arrange fried eggs on top of hash.

Pulling it all together: While eggs fry, toss mixed greens with the vinaigrette. Garnish hash with parsley. Serve and enjoy!

> **Did you know?!?** Grass-fed beef has more omega-3 fatty acids than farm raised Atlantic salmon? It's true! Adequate omega-3 intake reduces your risk of obesity, heart attack, stroke, ADHD, and autoimmune disease.

The next time I make this, I'm going to try..._____

My actual cooking times for this dish were..._____

I'm going to share this recipe with..._____

Asparagus and Spaghetti alla Carbonara

START TO FINISH: 30 MINUTES, MOSTLY ACTIVE

One of the most memorable restaurant dishes we've eaten was at Rancho Pinot in Scottsdale, Arizona: fresh asparagus topped with crispy pancetta, breadcrumbs, and a fried egg... ooey, gooey, goodness at its finest. Often referred to in Italy as "poor man's spaghetti", Spaghetti alla Carbonara is a traditional dish made with pasta, bacon, eggs, and cheese. Combining the two dishes seemed like a match made in heaven. Most versions of carbonara include added cream or oil to coat the noodles. After deciding that bacon provided enough fat and Parmigiano-Reggiano enough flavor, we eliminated the extra fat altogether. It turned out perfect!

8	oz spaghetti	½	cup Parmigiano-Reggiano, plus garnish
4	slices (¼ lb) nitrate-free bacon	2	eggs
½	cup diced red onion	½	tsp fresh ground black pepper
3	cloves garlic		Sea salt, to taste
1	bunch (1 lb) pencil thin asparagus		

Bacon and Parmigiano-Reggiano are both naturally salty. Taste your finished carbonara before adding any additional salt. You may find that it is completely unnecessary.

This is a great meal for the whole family! When I told Annie we were having bacon and egg noodles for dinner, her eyes lit up! She loved helping to whisk the eggs and pretending that the asparagus were ballerinas. If asparagus is not in season, substitute frozen. Vegetarians, while not at all traditional, could omit the bacon and sauté the onion and garlic in two tablespoons of melted butter. Asparagus and Spaghetti alla Carbonara is naturally nut-free, and could be gluten-free when prepared using quinoa spaghetti. This recipe serves three to four adults. The leftovers taste fine for a quick and easy lunch, but the texture of the sauce changes when reheated. Recipe may be doubled.

Instructions:

Prepare your ingredients: Dice ½ cup red onion (½ small, ¼ large, eyeball it). Mince 3 cloves garlic. Trim asparagus and, on the diagonal, slice into 1½ inch pieces. Use kitchen shears to cut 4 slices of nitrate-free bacon into ¼ inch slices. Whisk 2 eggs until very well beaten. Stir ½ cup grated (or shaved) Parmigiano-Reggiano into eggs.

> **Quick tip!!!** In order for the sauce to properly bind, it is important that everything finishes at the same time. I know that stovetops differ, but I've found that it works best to start heating my skillet when the pasta water just begins to simmer. Note what works for you below.

Prepare your spaghetti and asparagus: Cook 8 ounces of spaghetti in salted, boiling water one minute shy of package directions. When 3 minutes remain on the noodles, add the asparagus to the same pot. Before draining, reserve ½ cup pasta water. Drain, but do not rinse.

When pasta water is starting to simmer, start your bacon: Heat a large flat skillet over medium heat for about 5 minutes. Add sliced bacon and sauté for an additional 5 minutes. Add diced onion and garlic to bacon. Season with ½ tsp fresh ground black pepper and sauté 5 minutes more.

Pulling it all together: Return pasta and asparagus to the pot you prepared it in. Reduce heat to medium. Pour ¼ cup pasta water (not the whole ½ cup) and the combined bacon, onion, garlic, and pan drippings over noodles. Use tongs to toss continually for about 2 minutes, until all of the noodles are thoroughly coated with bacon drippings. **Remove pot from heat** (or your eggs will curdle). Pour egg and cheese sauce over coated noodles and toss continually for another 2 minutes, until sauce has reached a creamy, custardy consistency. If necessary, add the additional ¼ cup of pasta water 1 tbsp at a time. (This will depend on the water content of your eggs and cheese, sometimes I need it, sometimes I don't.) Salt and pepper to taste, and transfer to serving platter. Serve immediately and enjoy!

The next time I make this, I'm going to try..._____

My actual cooking times for this dish were..._____

I'm going to share this recipe with..._____

Coconut-Crusted Chicken Tenders
served alongside German potato salad

START TO FINISH: 40 MINUTES, 15 MINUTES ACTIVE

What's more American than fried chicken and potato salad? Maybe healthy baked chicken tenders and lower-calorie, vegetable packed potato salad? I think so, especially when the flavors are more complex and satisfying than the unhealthy, fatty versions. To make getting dinner on the table a snap, make the potato salad up to a day ahead! If you are feeling ambitious, bake a double batch of the chicken tenders and freeze the extras on a parchment paper lined baking sheet. Once frozen, transfer them to a labeled and dated freezer bag. On days that mealtime gets crazy, you will have a quick go-to lunch or dinner at a fraction of the cost of store bought chicken tenders.

For the chicken tenders:

1½	pounds chicken tenders	1	tsp sea salt
½	cup organic, shredded unsweetened coconut	1	tsp fresh ground black pepper
1	cup whole wheat panko breadcrumbs	1	egg
		1	tbsp Dijon mustard

For the potato salad:

1	pound red potatoes	3	stalks celery
2	hard-cooked eggs	½	cup diced red onion
3	slices nitrate-free bacon	¼	cup flat-leaf parsley

For the German dressing:

½	cup sour cream	½	tsp sea salt
½	tsp dried basil	¾	tsp fresh ground black pepper
½	tsp garlic salt		
¼	tsp celery salt		

This is a simple and comforting dinner that is perfect for those first post-winter, al fresco dinners. Our girls love this meal, and we feel good knowing that we are providing them a well-rounded, healthy dinner without depriving them of the basic "kid-foods". Vegetarians can use extra firm organic tofu sticks in place of the chicken, and omit the bacon from the salad. For a gluten-free meal, prepare using gluten-free bread crumbs. This dinner is naturally nut-free. Serves four to six.

Instructions:

Preheat oven to 350 degrees.

Bread your chicken: While oven heats, combine breadcrumbs, coconut, sea salt, and fresh ground black pepper in a small mixing or cereal sized bowl. In a second bowl, whisk together one egg with Dijon mustard. Dip each chicken tender into egg mixture and then thoroughly coat with the breading. Place breaded chicken tenders in a 13 x 9 inch glass baking dish (no added oil or fat needed!). Bake chicken for 20 – 25 minutes, until chicken reaches an internal temperature of 160 - 165 degrees. Remove from oven and let rest for about 5 minutes. This will bring the chicken to 165+ degrees (the temperature needed to kill food borne bacteria) without drying out your chicken.

Prepare all ingredients for the potato salad: As soon as the chicken goes in the oven, cover one pound of red potatoes with water plus two inches. Boil potatoes for about 20 minutes, until fork tender but not mushy. While potatoes cook, trim and thinly slice 3 stalks celery. Dice ½ of a red onion (about ½ to ¾ cup), and coarsely chop ¼ cup flat leaf parsley. If necessary, prepare 2 hard cooked eggs and fry 3 slices of nitrate-free bacon. Once cooled, dice eggs and crumble bacon. Place all ingredients in a large mixing bowl.

Prepare your German dressing and toss your potato salad: Whisk together all ingredients listed under "for the German dressing".

Pulling it all together: When potatoes are cool enough to handle (you can speed the process by emerging them in a bowl of ice water after boiling), dice into ½ inch bites (a serrated knife works best to cut through the skins). Add potatoes to other salad ingredients. Pour dressing over top and toss thoroughly to combine. Serve alongside your coconut crusted chicken tenders and your family's favorite dipping sauce. (Reminder: the potato salad can be made up to a day ahead.)

> **Did you know?** Using sour cream instead of mayonnaise in this potato salad saves you about 650 calories and 60 grams of fat!

The next time I make this, I'm going to try..._____

My actual cooking times for this dish were..._____

I'm going to share this recipe with..._____

Leek, Wild Rice, and Mushroom Soup
served with your family's favorite quick bread

START TO FINISH: 1 HOUR, 20 MINUTES. 20 MINUTES ACTIVE

My friend, Heather, shared a version of this recipe with me just shortly after my family moved to Kansas City. (Before my crazy leek story, I must say that the cream-free version of this soup turned out awesome, and is a great comfort food on a chilly spring evening.) When I read the email that inspired this recipe, it was a cold, rainy day and I immediately decided to make this soup for dinner that night. After stopping at the store for leeks and mushrooms (everything else is a staple), I headed to the kitchen. I had never worked with leeks before, but I figured they were basically big scallions. They are not. Learn from me! The dark green part of a leek is bitter and yucky. Really yucky. Once you get through the white and pale green parts, send the rest to the compost pile! We made it through my first attempt, deciding the soup had a good enough flavor that we would try it again using leeks the proper way. It was a winner!

2	leeks, white and pale green parts only	2	tbsp extra virgin olive oil
1	pound sliced white mushrooms	1	tbsp butter
2	cloves garlic	2	tbsp corn starch
1	small onion	1	tsp dried thyme
½	cup wild rice, uncooked	½	tsp dried basil
5	cups chicken broth	½	tsp sea salt + to taste
¼	cup dry sherry	½	tsp fresh ground black pepper
⅔	cup whole milk	¼	tsp ground cayenne

While this soup tastes rich and decadent, it is actually very light. Whatever quick bread you love the most (pumpkin, poppy seed, blueberry), make several loaves at once to freeze for busy nights. Be sure to use whole grains! Pureeing the veggies makes this dish toddler friendly, and is a great way to introduce new flavors like leeks. Vegetarians can substitute vegetable broth for the chicken broth. This soup is naturally gluten-free and nut-free.

Instructions:

Prep your produce: Dice 1 small onion. Chop 3 cloves garlic. Thinly slice 2 leeks, white and pale green parts only. Thinly slice mushrooms, if necessary. Reserve a few leek rings and mushroom slices for garnish.

Sauté your vegetables: Heat a large pot or Dutch oven over medium heat for about 5 minutes. When hot, add 2 tbsp extra virgin olive oil and 1 tbsp butter. When butter has melted, add leeks, onion, and garlic to pot. Season with ½ tsp each sea salt and black pepper. Let the veggies cook down for about 8 minutes, stirring occasionally. Add mushrooms and sauté 3 minutes longer. Turn heat to low and add 1 cup chicken broth. Use an immersion blender to coarsely puree soup (this takes about a minute). Alternatively, transfer to a blender or food processor.

Simmer your soup: If necessary, return vegetables to pot. Add ¼ cup dry sherry, remaining quart chicken broth, ½ cup (uncooked) wild rice, 1 tsp dried thyme, ½ tsp dried basil, and ¼ tsp ground cayenne to the vegetable mixture. Increase heat to bring soup just to a boil. Reduce heat to medium-low. Half cover pot with lid and simmer for 1 hour.

Getting it on the table: When soup has finished simmering and the rice has popped and curled (this will make sense when it happens), whisk 2 tbsp corn starch into ⅔ cup milk. Stir milk mixture into soup. Turn off heat and adjust seasonings, if necessary. Ladle soup into bowls, and garnish with reserved leeks and mushrooms. Serve and enjoy!

> **Quick tip!!!** I almost always make a double batch of soups and stews. I freeze the second batch in a labeled and dated freezer bag, and then lay it flat in my freezer. On nights that I'm too busy (or tired) to cook, it is comforting to know that I have a great, homemade soup on hand to feed my family!

The next time I make this, I'm going to try..._____

My actual cooking times for this dish were..._____

I'm going to share this recipe with..._____

Chicken and Mushroom Marsala
on a simple bed of parsleyed egg noodles

START TO FINISH: 25 MINUTES, MOSTLY ACTIVE

When creating recipes, we often turn to restaurant menus for inspiration. One would assume that if people are going to spend their hard earned money to eat overpriced cuisine, it must be good. Additionally, restaurant chefs prepare the meals ahead of time or relatively quickly once the order is in. One menu item that seems to appear again and again is Chicken Marsala. After perfecting the "healthified" version of this recipe, our family understands why. Chicken Marsala is delicious! Original versions contain up to a stick of butter. We were finally able to reduce it to just one tablespoon without compromising the consistency of the sauce. This is a quick and savory restaurant quality meal that is easy to whip together on even the busiest of weeknights.

For the chicken and mushroom marsala:

1	pound boneless, skinless chicken breasts	½	cup Marsala wine
8	oz cremini mushrooms	2	tbsp extra virgin olive oil
1	cup chicken broth	1	tbsp butter

For the breading:

¼	cup unbleached all purpose flour	½	tsp sea salt
2	tsp salt-free Italian seasoning blend	½	tsp fresh ground black pepper
½	tsp garlic powder	1	egg

For the parsleyed egg noodles:

3½	cups egg noodles (⅓ standard pkg)	1	tbsp extra virgin olive oil
½	cup flat leaf parsley. plus more to garnish	½	tsp garlic salt

After many attempts at achieving the results I was after, no one in my family ever complained about having to eat this meal over and over. That's huge! Vegetarians can omit the chicken, double the mushrooms, and add all of the flour mixture to vegetable broth. If sensitive to gluten, use gluten-free rice flour and substitute brown rice fusilli for the egg noodles. This dish is nut-free. Serves four.

Ingredients:

Prepare your ingredients: Coarsely chop ½ cup + 2 tbsp parsley. Quarter mushrooms. Crack egg into a small bowl and whisk until scrambled. In a second bowl, combine all remaining ingredients listed under "for the breading".

Pound out your chicken: Cut chicken into eight similar sized pieces (two small medallions per person is more aesthetically pleasing than one large one). Place chicken between 2 pieces of wax paper and use a rolling pin or the flat side of a meat tenderizer to pound chicken until it is about ¼ to ½ inch thick.

Prepare your parsleyed egg noodles: Cook egg noodles in salted, boiling water according to package directions. Drain and return to pan. Toss egg noodles with 1 tbsp extra virgin olive oil, ½ cup flat leaf parsley, and ½ tsp garlic salt.

While your pasta water heats, prepare your Marsala: Heat a large flat skillet over medium high heat for about 5 minutes. When skillet is hot, add 2 tbsp extra virgin olive oil. Dip each piece of chicken into the scrambled egg and then coat with the herbed flour mixture. Place chicken cutlets in pan and brown for 3 – 4 minutes per side. DO NOT DISCARD REMAINING FLOUR MIXTURE! When chicken is browned and cooked through, transfer to a clean plate to rest. Add the mushrooms, ½ cup Marsala wine, and 1 tbsp butter to the now empty skillet. Stir to incorporate any brown bits of flavor left from the chicken. Continue to sauté mushrooms for 5 minutes or until almost all of the liquid has evaporated. Add remaining herbed flour mixture and 1 cup chicken broth to mushrooms. Stir continuously for 3 – 5 minutes, until the sauce has been reduced by about half. Return chicken to skillet and spoon Marsala sauce over chicken to coat. After 1 – 2 minutes have lapsed, chicken will be hot and ready to serve.

Pulling it all together: For an impressive presentation, pour parsleyed egg noodles onto a suitable sized platter plate. Use tongs to arrange chicken cutlets on the bed of noodles. Spoon mushrooms and all remaining sauce over platter, and garnish with additional parsley.

The next time I make this dish, I want to try..._____

My actual cooking times for this dish were..._____

I'm going to share this recipe with..._____

Classic Bolognese

START TO FINISH: 5 – 6 HOURS, 1 HOUR ACTIVE

Bolognese (or ragu alla Bolognese) is a rich meaty pasta sauce that originated in the city of Bologna in northern Italy. It is inexpensive to make, tastes delicious, and is a great way to feed a crowd. You do spend an hour in the kitchen, but once all of the ingredients are incorporated, you set the pot to simmer and walk away for the rest of the afternoon. Bolognese is one of our family's favorite meals to make when entertaining friends for Sunday supper. When guests arrive, the house smells fantastic and the only thing left to do is boil some pasta and toss a salad! Alternatively, this meal is great to serve on nights that will be crazy. The sauce can be pulled together while the kids are at school or napping, and then left alone to simmer until everyone has a chance to sit down together. Using such a generous amount of vegetables also makes this a perfect one-dish meal! This recipe makes enough for at least eight hungry adults. If your family is small like ours, prepare just half a box of noodles, and freeze half of the sauce for a future meal. Properly frozen and defrosted, this sauce will taste fresh for at least three months.

3	slices nitrate-free bacon	3	ribs celery, diced
2	tbsp extra virgin olive oil	4	cloves garlic, minced
1	large red onion	1	tsp sea salt
3	carrots, diced	1	tsp fresh ground black pepper

1	lb grass-fed ground beef	½	tsp nutmeg
¾	cup whole milk	1	cup red wine

28	oz can peeled tomatoes	3	sprigs fresh thyme
28	oz can crushed tomatoes	1	lemon, zest and juice
		½	tsp crushed red pepper

1   pound pipe rigate noodles
½   cup Parmigiano-Reggiano, plus more for passing

Instructions:

Prepare your soffritto: "Soffritto" is an Italian word that refers to the base of many Italian dishes. It traditionally contains onion, carrots, celery, and garlic. So, to prepare your soffritto, dice 1 large red onion, 3 carrots, and 3 ribs of celery. Mince 4 cloves garlic. Set aside.

Start your sauce: Heat a large stockpot or Dutch oven over medium heat for about 5 minutes. While the pot heats, use your kitchen shears to cut 3 slices of bacon into ¼ inch strips. When pot is hot, add bacon and brown for about 7 minutes. After 7 minutes have lapsed, add 2 tbsp extra virgin olive oil and your soffritto to the bacon. Season with 1 tsp each sea salt and fresh ground black pepper. Sauté for about 12 minutes, until veggies are tender and onion translucent.

Incorporate your meat: When veggies are tender and 12 minutes have lapsed, add ground beef to pot. Brown beef for about 4 minutes. Next, stir in ¾ cup milk and ½ tsp ground nutmeg. Simmer for an additional 12 minutes, stirring regularly to encourage the beef to absorb the milk. Add 1 cup red wine and ½ cup water. Simmer/boil (still over medium heat) for 25 minutes. At this point, you will only need to stir occasionally to prevent the sauce from sticking to the bottom.

Final step, then walk away: While wine is simmering, coarsely chop peeled tomatoes, and then return them to their juice. Coarsely chop 2 – 3 sprigs of fresh thyme, leaves and tender stems only. When the 25 minutes have lapsed, add peeled tomatoes, crushed tomatoes, chopped thyme, ½ tsp crushed red pepper, and the zest and juice of one lemon. Bring sauce just to a boil and then reduce heat between low to medium-low (so it will just barely be simmering). Gently simmer for 4 to 6 hours. If your liquid seems to be evaporating too quickly, turn your heat down a notch farther and add an additional ¼ cup of water.

Pulling it all together: 30 minutes before you want to eat, begin to heat the water for your pasta. Cook pasta in salted, boiling water for time indicated on package. Drain, rinse with cool water, and return to pot. Ladle the desired amount of sauce over noodles and toss to combine. Pour Bolognese into a large serving bowl and garnish with ¼ - ½ cup Parmigiano-Reggiano cheese. If desired, serve Bolognese with crusty bread, a simple green salad, and additional Parmigiano-Reggiano. Enjoy! (continued on next page)

Traditionally, Bolognese is served with pappardelle or fettuccine noodles. We like to use pipe rigate (or another ridged tubular pasta) because it clings to the sauce better, and the airy noodles add bulk to the dish (making portions appear larger). Use whichever you prefer. Everyone that we've shared this dinner with loves it, is surprised that it is healthy, and is impressed that the sauce is made from scratch! Vegetarians should substitute non-GMO soy crumbles for the ground beef and omit the bacon. To provide enough fat for sautéing the soffritto, you will need to add 2 tbsp of butter when you heat the olive oil. When ladled over gluten-free pasta, this dish is naturally gluten-free. It is also free of nuts or any nut products.

The next time I make this, I'm going to try..._____

My actual cooking times for this recipe were..._____

I'm going to share this recipe with..._____

Cooking with wine for kids: I am often asked my opinion on using wine as a seasoning in meals intended for children. Studies have shown that up to 95% of the alcohol in a dish evaporates during the cooking process. Therefore, I serve all of my recipes to Annie and Ellie with no reservations. However, if the alcohol has not been heated (as in some fruit desserts), or if the alcohol is stirred into the recipe at the very end (without allowing time for it to evaporate), I choose to take our family's dinner in a different direction. I consider all recipes in this cookbook to be perfectly safe for children.

The First Four

When making any significant lifestyle change, it is easy to become overwhelmed and quit. Switching to "real food" eating is no different. Remember that I began exploring the world of holistic eating over 10 years before I decided to publish this book. You are not trying to live life perfectly; you are simply trying to eat better today than you did the day before. When people ask me the best way to start making the transition to real food, I always tell them to start by reading labels and eliminating "The First Four". The first four ingredients that I recommend eliminating are high fructose corn syrup, hydrogenated oils, artificial colors, and artificial sweeteners. Just because something sounds healthy or is labeled "all natural" does not mean that it is. The easiest way to quickly improve your family's diet is to scan labels and avoid foods that contain the following words: **hydrogenated, partially hydrogenated, high fructose corn syrup, red no. __, yellow no. __, blue no. __, sucralose (Splenda), and aspartame.** All of these ingredients are synthetically produced and offer no nutritional benefits whatsoever. In fact, quite the contrary! Studies conducted throughout the world have shown that consuming these dangerous chemicals increase your chance of developing heart disease, cancer, diabetes, obesity, infertility, kidney disease, liver disease, hyperactivity, ADD/ADHD, autoimmune disease, migraines, and more. If these foods are so controversial, you may be wondering why food manufacturers put them in our food. They are cheap, increase a product's shelf life, and they make fake food more visually appealing. Do you really want to eat a granola bar that is older than your toddler or eat artificially colored strawberry flavored fruit snacks instead of fresh strawberries? I truly believe that if you eliminate or drastically reduce these ingredients from your diet, you will have more energy, feel better, look better, and enjoy fewer health complications throughout your life.

Chicken and Mango Thai Salad

START TO FINISH: 10 MINUTES!!!

This is one of our family's favorite dinners for busy nights! Using precooked chicken takes this main dish salad from start to finish in less than 10 minutes. The sweetness of the antioxidant rich mango contrasts perfectly with the immunity boosting red onion and bell pepper. The celery gives it a refreshing crunch, and the chicken is packed with lean protein. This fun and easy salad is finished with a quick toss in a homemade walnut vinaigrette. It's satisfying, nourishing, and downright tasty! This recipe makes four generous servings. If you are a smaller family, only dress half of the salad ingredients for tonight's dinner. Store the remaining vinaigrette separate from the remaining salad ingredients for up to three days.

For the salad:

3	cups diced, cooked chicken (or shredded)	1	red bell pepper
4	ribs celery	1	bunch cilantro
1	mango	½	cup peanuts
1	red onion	6	cups romaine lettuce

For the walnut vinaigrette:

¼	cup walnut oil	2	tbsp fish sauce
3	limes, juiced	2	cloves garlic, minced
2	tbsp sesame oil	½	tsp crushed red pepper
2	tbsp organic sugar		

Fish sauce is a popular Asian condiment that is available in the Asian section of most major grocery stores, Asian markets, and online. This dish is naturally gluten-free, but double check the ingredients on your fish sauce. Those sensitive to nuts can omit the peanuts and substitute extra virgin olive oil for the walnut oil. I'm sorry vegetarians, I do not know of a vegetarian replacement for fish sauce. If you have found one, please let me know!

Instructions:

Prep your produce: Dice red onion, bell pepper, mango, and celery. Chop romaine lettuce. Coarsely chop one bunch of cilantro. Combine in a mixing bowl with the peanuts and chicken. If you are prepping your ingredients ahead of time, wait to chop the cilantro until you are ready to serve. When it is removed from the stem it will almost immediately begins to wilt.

Prepare your vinaigrette: Measure and whisk together all ingredients listed under "for the walnut vinaigrette".

Pulling it all together: Arrange the chopped romaine on a platter plate. Toss the prepared ingredients with the vinaigrette according to your preference (you may have extra dressing). Serve and enjoy!

Kids can cook! Because there is no raw meat involved, this dish is great for little helpers. I like to prepare the vinaigrette and chop all of the ingredients during naptime. I then refrigerate them all in separate bowls on the shelf that is at Annie's eye level. When it is time to eat, we get out a mixing bowl and let Annie "cook" the whole dinner, picking her ingredients from the fridge one at a time. We then take turns tossing the salad. I truly believe one of the reasons she loves this salad so much is because she has so much fun preparing it!

The next time I make this, I'm going to try..._____

My actual cooking times for this dish were..._____

I'm going to share this recipe with..._____

Dinners for Summer

Orecchiette with Tuna, Fennel, and Arugula

Ginger-Peach Chicken & Creamy Eggplant Lentils

Greek Chicken, Veggie and Orzo Pilaf

Chicken Pad Thai

Crock Pot Carnitas

Moily Haldi, Sri Lanka Street Food

Black Bean & Corn Enchilada Pie

Chicken, Cherry & Red Bean Curry

Roasted Tomato Pesto Pasta

Roasted Chicken Mandarin Orange Salad

Broccolini and Chicken Sausage Penne

Seared Scallops Triple Corn Polenta

Orecchiette with Fennel, Tuna, and Arugula

START TO FINISH: 25 MINUTES, 15 MINUTES ACTIVE

When eaten in moderation, canned tuna is a great way to stretch your family's food dollar. In this tasty summer supper, tuna, fennel, and arugula come together to create a simple yet complex meal the whole family is sure to love. The bright flavors of the fennel and lemon mix with creamy cottage cheese to balance the flavor of the bold tuna. This makes it super kid-friendly! Served warm or at room temperature, this flavorful and nutrient packed dish is the perfect meal for your next al fresco dinner! Serves four to six.

8	ounces orecchiette pasta (1/2 package)	4	cups arugula, (5-ounce package)
2	6-ounce cans tuna, light chunk in water, undrained	1	lemon, zest and juice
1	fennel bulb	2	tbsp Parmigiano-Reggiano
1	red onion	2	tbsp extra virgin olive oil
3	cloves garlic	1	tsp sea salt
1	cup cottage cheese	½	tsp black pepper
¼	cup pine nuts		

After telling Annie that orecchiette translates to "pig ear" pasta, she fell in love with this meal. We love that it introduces the girls to interesting flavors like tuna, fennel, and arugula. Does she gobble up the arugula and ask for more? Not yet, but she will. Don't get discouraged if your kids don't like something the first time you offer it. Keep trying. In the meantime, be proud of this tasty meal you prepared from scratch, and feel good knowing your kids are eating real food, not preservatives! Vegetarians can omit the tuna and double the cottage cheese, adding ¼ cup of water with the fennel. Those sensitive to gluten only need to substitute gluten-free pasta, and those with nut allergies can substitute pepitas (toasted pumpkin seeds) or sunflower seeds for the pine nuts.

Instructions:

Cook the orecchiette: Bring a large pot of salted boiling water to a rolling boil. Add orecchiette and cook for the time indicated on package. Drain and immediately rinse with cool water to stop the cooking process. Drain again. Let orecchiette rest in colander until ready to use.

Quick tip!!! Do not drain your tuna! If you accidentally buy the pouches or drain your cans before reading this, add ¼ cup filtered water at the same time you add the tuna to the skillet. Be sure to make a note below so that you don't make the same mistake again.

While the water heats, prep your produce: Dice 1 onion and 3 cloves garlic. Core, trim, and thinly slice fennel bulb, reserving 2 tbsp of the fronds (the little grassy things, not the big stalk) for your garnish. Open cans of tuna, but do not drain.

When orecchiette goes into the water, start your sauté: Heat a large deep skillet over medium high heat for about 5 minutes. When hot, add 2 tbsp extra virgin olive oil and heat an additional 30 seconds, until oil shimmers. Place onion, garlic, and pine nuts in skillet, and sauté for 2 minutes. Next, add the tuna and juices to skillet. Season with 1 tsp sea salt and ½ tsp freshly ground black pepper. Sauté one minute more. Finally, add fennel to tuna mixture. Cover skillet with a tight fitting lid and simmer for 2 – 3 minutes, until fennel is soft but still crisp tender. Turn off heat.

Bringing it all together: Return orecchiette to cooking pot. Top with 4 cups arugula, 1 cup cottage cheese, and the zest and juice of one lemon. Pour tuna and fennel mixture into pot. Toss to combine and to slightly wilt arugula. Transfer to a serving dish and garnish with reserved fennel fronds and Parmigiano-Reggiano. Serve and enjoy!

The next time I make this, I'm going to try..._____

My actual cooking times for this dish were..._____

I'm going to share this recipe with..._____

Ginger-Peach Chicken Skewers
on a bed of creamy eggplant lentils

START TO FINISH: 70 MINUTES, 20 MINUTES ACTIVE

I am so thankful that I have had the opportunity to get to know Cheryl Greene. She is part of the genius-ness behind drgreene.com and an inspiring woman (so is his daughter, Claire). If you haven't checked this website out, you should! Cheryl is one of the many vegetarians married to a carnivore loving spouse. She absolutely inspired this dish. The lentils are a great vegetarian main dish for Cheryl and Claire, while the chicken adds the meat factor for the boys. If you are like our family, and love it all, the medley of the two is heavenly and a great way to use summer's bounty of produce.

For the ginger-peach chicken:

1	pound boneless, skinless chicken breast	½	tsp ground mustard
2	ripe juicy peaches	½	tsp mild curry powder
½	cup filtered water	½	tsp sea salt
1	tbsp + 1 tsp pure honey	½	tsp fresh ground black pepper
½	tsp ground ginger	1	tsp apple cider vinegar

For the creamy eggplant lentils:

1	Japanese or other heirloom eggplant, ½ lb	2	ounces cream cheese
1	red onion	½	bunch cilantro
6	cloves garlic	2	tsp ground cumin
1	cup dried lentils	¼	tsp ground nutmeg
2	cups vegetable broth	½	tsp sea salt
1	tbsp extra virgin olive oil	½	tsp fresh ground black pepper

> Using ripe peaches is the key to making this sweet and savory sauce with the smallest amounts of added sugars. If your peaches have not fully ripened, you will need to add an additional two teaspoons of honey to your sauce.

This is the ultimate in kid-friendly dishes. When Annie heard she was getting peach chicken on a stick for dinner, she started jumping up and down. Before Ellie turned one, she just enjoyed the lentils (no honey for babies). Vegetarians can omit the chicken, and stir the ginger-peach sauce into the finished lentils. This dinner is naturally gluten-free and nut-free. Serves four.

Instructions:

Prep your produce: Dice 2 ripe peaches into ¼ to ½ inch pieces. Set aside. Cube 1 heirloom eggplant. Dice 1 large red onion, reserving ¼ cup. Mince 6 cloves garlic.

Start your lentils: In a small bowl or ramekin, combine 2 tsp ground cumin, ¼ tsp ground nutmeg, and ½ tsp each sea salt and black pepper. Heat a medium sized saucepan over medium heat for about 5 minutes. When hot, add 1 tbsp extra virgin olive oil and heat an additional 30 seconds, until oil shimmers. Add eggplant, onion (minus the reserved ¼ cup), and garlic to skillet. Sauté for about 3 minutes. Add combined seasonings and stir continuously for 2 minutes, being mindful not to let the spices burn. When 2 minutes have lapsed, add 3 cups vegetable broth and 1 cup dried lentils to the pot. Increase heat to bring mixture just to a boil. Reduce heat to medium low and simmer uncovered for one hour, until most of the liquid has been absorbed.

When lentils begin simmering, prepare your seasoning paste for the chicken and skewer your chicken: In a small bowl or ramekin, combine ½ tsp each of ground ginger, ground mustard, curry powder, sea salt, and freshly ground black pepper. Stir in 1 tsp apple cider vinegar to form a paste. Use kitchen shears or a sharp knife to cut chicken into 1-inch bites. Divide among four wooden or reusable skewers.

Prepare your ginger-peach sauce: Heat a small saucepan over medium heat for about 2 minutes. Add diced peaches, ½ cup water, and 1 tbsp + 1 tsp honey to saucepan. Simmer over medium heat for about 8 minutes, stirring occasionally. When you stir the sauce, use the back of your wooden spoon to break down the peaches. After 8 minutes have lapsed, add the seasoning paste to saucepan and stir continuously for 2 minutes more. This allows the flavor in the spices to release and infuse the sauce. Be mindful not to let the spices burn. Remove from heat. (This can be done up to a day ahead and refrigerated until ready to use.)

Bake your chicken: Preheat oven to 350 degrees. While oven heats, brush your chicken skewers with half of the ginger-peach sauce and place in a 13 x 9 inch glass baking dish. Place in oven and bake for 20 minutes, or until chicken has reached an internal temperature of 160 degrees. Turn on broiler and broil the chicken for 2 minutes, to give the sauce a nice char. Remove from oven and let rest for about 5 minutes. (The 2 minutes in the broiler and the 5 minute rest time will bring the chicken up to 165+ degrees. This is the temperature chicken must reach in order to kill the bacteria that can cause food poisoning.)

Finish off your lentils: Coarsely chop ½ bunch of cilantro, leaves and tender stems only. When lentils have finished simmering, turn off heat. Stir in cream cheese, cilantro, and remaining onion.

Getting it on the table: Place a bed of lentils on each plate. Top with a ginger-peach chicken skewer. Place remaining sauce in small bowls for dipping.

Why you should never serve honey to babies:

Botulinum spores, which naturally exist in honey, can cause infant botulism when given to babies. Infant botulism is a rare, but possibly fatal disease that can cause muscle weakness and paralysis. This is the only health food that Annie and Ellie did not eat before 15 months. (I waited an extra three months just in case.) I gave them all of the other common allergens, but no honey! The problem is that babies under the age of one still have an immature gastrointestinal tract. Long story short, their little bodies can't process it; the botulism begins to multiply and their bodies become toxic. Botulism is also often misdiagnosed until it has become severe. At this point, the NICU is almost always involved. If your baby becomes sick and you accidentally gave her honey, please be honest with your pediatrician. This could save your baby's life.

Don't write honey off forever though! It is known throughout the world for its many health benefits. Honey tastes great drizzled over oatmeal, stirred into hot tea or coffee, or melted with peanut butter to create a healthy dip for whole grain pretzels and apples.

The next time I make this, I want to try..._____

My actual cooking times for this dish were..._____

I'm going to share this recipe with..._____

Greek Chicken, Vegetable, and Orzo Pilaf

START TO FINISH: 15 MINUTES, 10 MINUTES ACTIVE

When the weather heats up, this is a great dish to throw together on nights that you are craving something cool. Tangy yogurt, cooked chicken, and summer veggies come together to create a quick and healthful meal that the whole family is sure to enjoy! This salad can also be made up to a day ahead. On hectic days, it is so nice to know that I will have a well rounded, one dish dinner to serve my family when we finally get home!

1	cup orzo pasta	14	-16 ounces Greek yogurt (some brands sell different sizes)
1	cucumber		
1	pint cherry or grape tomatoes	1	tsp celery salt
2	cups cooked, shredded chicken (about ½ lb)	½	tsp seasoning salt
		½	tsp fresh ground black pepper
¼	cup kalamata olives		

Cook orzo according to package directions. When cooking time is complete, drain and immediately rinse with cool water (to stop the cooking process). When cool, drain again, very thoroughly.

While orzo cooks, dice veggies and combine yogurt with 1 tsp celery salt, ½ tsp seasoned salt, and ½ tsp fresh ground pepper.

Transfer cooked and rinsed orzo to a large mixing bowl, and toss with seasoned yogurt and prepared veggies. If desired, garnish with additional red onion and olives.

Did you know? Using 2% Greek yogurt instead of mayo in this salad saves you about 2,600 calories and 300 grams of fat! Vegetarians can omit the chicken. This dish is naturally free of nuts or nut products, and those sensitive to gluten can simply substitute brown rice pasta for the orzo. (Any pasta shape will work.)

The next time I make this, I'm going to try..._____

My actual cooking times for this dish were..._____

I'm going to share this recipe with..._____

Chicken Pad Thai

START TO FINISH: 25 – 30 MINUTES, ALL ACTIVE.

I love Chicken Pad Thai. Unfortunately, when ordered at a restaurant, you run the risk of consuming a full day's worth of fat, calories, and sodium in just one setting. Awhile back, we decided it was time for a pad Thai makeover. It turned out super tasty! We were a little worried that the sauce would be too hot for our little girls, but the honey really balanced the heat. They both gobbled it up! Another great thing about this recipe is that the whole thing, except for chopping the cilantro (it will wilt) can be prepped up to a day ahead. When the weather gets hot, I like to get my dinner prep work done during the heat of the afternoon. This gives me more evening time to spend outside with my family.

For the pad thai:

8	ounces rice (aka glass) noodles	1	red bell pepper
1	- 1½ cups cooked, shredded chicken	2	carrots
		1	small red onion
		2	cups bean sprouts

For the peanut-honey pad thai sauce:

¼	cup rice wine vinegar	1	tbsp sesame oil
2	tbsp organic peanut butter	½	tsp Sriracha chili sauce
1	inch piece of fresh ginger	1	tsp garlic salt
2	cloves garlic	1	tsp organic sugar
1	tbsp + 1 tsp honey	¼	tsp crushed red pepper, or more if you're daring
2	tsp soy sauce		

For the garnishments:

2	green onions	¼	cup roasted peanuts
¼	cup cilantro leaves		Lime wedges, for squeezing

Leftover pad thai gets watery, so we adjusted this recipe to generously feed two adults and two small children. I say "generously" because we all went in for seconds (thirds). This pad thai turned out that well. When made without the chicken, this dish is naturally vegetarian (and vegan)! When made with gluten-free soy sauce, it is naturally gluten-free. Those sensitive to nuts, try using sunflower seed butter instead of the peanut butter, and toasted sesame seeds in place of the peanuts. Feel free to add Sriracha!

Preparations:

Slicing and dicing: Peel and coarsely chop 3 cloves garlic and a 1-inch piece of ginger. Thinly slice 1 red onion. Core, seed, and thinly slice 1 red bell pepper. Peel and matchstick (or julienne) 2 carrots. Thinly slice 2 green onions.

Prepare the peanut-honey pad thai sauce: In a mini food processor (or blender), combine all ingredients listed under "for the peanut-honey pad thai sauce".

Cook rice noodles: In a pot of salted, boiling water, cook rice noodles according to package directions. Drain and immediately rinse with cold water until cooled to stop the cooking process. Failing to properly cool noodles will result in a yucky, mushy pad thai. If not directly stir frying the vegetables, toss noodles with 1 tsp sesame oil to prevent noodles from sticking. These noodles can be refrigerated up to 3 days or rest on the countertop for up to 2 hours.

Instructions:

Make your pad thai: Heat a large deep skillet (or wok) over medium high heat for about 5 minutes. Add 1 tbsp extra virgin olive oil and heat an additional 30 seconds, until oil shimmers. Add thinly sliced onion and stir fry for 2 minutes. Next, add carrots and stir fry for 1 – 2 minutes more. Finally, add the bell pepper and stir fry 1 minute longer. Reduce heat to medium low. Stir in bean sprouts, cooked shredded chicken, cooked rice noodles, and pad thai sauce. Toss until chicken and noodles are warm and to distribute sauce throughout. Transfer contents of skillet to serving dish, squeeze with lime wedges, and garnish with green onions, cilantro, and peanuts. If desired, pass Sriracha and additional lime wedges at the table. Serve and enjoy!

Ingredient tip!!! When selecting your rice wine vinegar, be sure that you DO NOT choose the "seasoned" variety. Seasoned rice wine vinegar has added sugars and spices that will throw off the delicate balance of sweet, spicy, and sour this pad Thai delivers.

The next time I make this, I want to try..._____

My actual cooking times for this dish were..._____

I'm going to share this recipe with..._____

Crock Pot Carnitas
with cilantro-lime red cabbage and fresh avocado

START TO FINISH: 6½ HOURS, 30 MINUTES ACTIVE

This is the perfect dinner to share with family and friends on a hot summer night. The crock pot does almost all of the work for you, keeping your kitchen (and your house) cool as a cucumber. Because almost the entire meal can be prepped hours ahead, you can spend your evening outdoors, enjoying the fresh air rather than trapped inside cooking. The pureed chipotle in adobo gives the tender pork just a bit of heat and totally compliments the citrus-y cabbage. We like to serve these carnitas with fruit fresh from the farmer's market. Serves four to six.

For the carnitas:

1	- 1¼ pound pork tenderloin	1	tbsp cumin
1	small red onion	1½	tsp chili powder
2	cloves garlic	1	tsp pureed canned chipotle in adobo
¾	cup white wine	½	tsp sea salt
2	tbsp white wine vinegar	¼	tsp black pepper

For the cilantro-lime cream sauce:

1	cup sour cream	½	tsp sea salt
2	limes, zest and juice	½	tsp fresh ground black pepper
½	cup chopped cilantro		
3	green onions		

Additional ingredients:
Avocadoes, ½ per person
Red cabbage, ¼ -½ head, shredded, 4 – 6 cups
Corn tortillas, 2 per person
Seasonal fresh fruit, about a cup per person

I'll admit that I was nervous serving toddlers chipotle in adobo, but they loved it all (even nibbling on a few shreds of cabbage)! When prepared with 100% corn tortillas (read the label), this dish is naturally gluten-free and nut-free. Vegetarians, cook three cups of prepared white beans (or two 15-ounce cans, rinsed and drained) in place of the pork. Mash the beans and braising liquid together, smear over a corn tortilla, and serve tostado style topped with avocado, cabbage, and garnishments.

Instructions:

Prepare your carnitas: About 6½ hours before you would like to serve dinner, dice 1 small red onion and 2 cloves garlic. Place in the bottom of a medium to large slow cooker. If necessary, puree canned chipotle in adobo. Add 1 tsp of pureed chipotle, pork tenderloin, and all remaining ingredients listed under "for the carnitas" to the slow cooker. Cover and cook carnitas over lowest setting for about 6 hours.

> **Quick tip!!!** When you open a can of chipotle in adobo, puree the whole thing. On a parchment lined baking sheet, drop pureed adobo in 1 tsp increments and freeze. When frozen, transfer to a labeled and dated freezer bag. Properly frozen, these taste fresh for four to six months and are a great smoky ingredient to have on hand. 3 teaspoons of puree equals 1 whole chipotle.

Prepare your cilantro-lime cream sauce: Thinly slice 2 green onions. Reserve 1 – 2 tbsp for garnish, and then mince the remainder. Chop ½ cup fresh cilantro. In a small bowl, combine minced green onion, cilantro, and all remaining ingredients listed under "for the cilantro-lime cream sauce". Refrigerate until ready to use.

Bringing it all together: About 30 minutes before you would like to serve dinner, heat a large flat skillet over medium high heat. While skillet heats, core and thinly slice ¼ to ½ head red cabbage, about 4 to 6 cups. Toss shredded cabbage with about ½ of the cilantro-lime cream sauce. Use two forks or wooden spoons to shred pork tenderloin. Turn off crock pot and allow pork to stand for 10 - 15 minutes to absorb the juices. While pork rests, begin to "fry" tortillas in hot, dry skillet for about a minute per side. Cover hot tortillas with a damp paper towel.

Getting it on the table: Just before serving, slice each avocado half into 4 slices. Coarsely chop an additional ¼ - ½ cup of cilantro. Place about ¼ cup each of pork mixture and cabbage into each tortilla. Garnish each taco with 2 slices of avocado and a sprinkling of cilantro. Repeat until each guest has two tacos. Divide remaining cream sauce among plates and garnish with reserved red onion.

The next time I make this, I'm going to try..._____

My actual cooking times for this dish were..._____

I'm going to share this recipe with..._____

Moily Haldi
A Sri Lankan street food

START TO FINISH: 45 MINUTES, 25 MINUTES ACTIVE

I read cookbooks the way most people read novels. I just love the stories and history behind food and where it came from. One of my favorites is <u>Street Food</u> by Tom Kime. Mr. Kime traveled to 15 countries, feasting on the food sold at open-air markets, roadside stands, and local cafes; street food. After talking to the chefs, he wrote stories and recipes that allow us to experience his journeys from the comfort of our own homes. While most of the food Mr. Kime shares is a bit too "exquisite" for our little family, the flavor combinations he experienced throughout the world have definitely inspired some of our best recipes. The recipe I share below is our user friendly, family friendly adaptation of Moily Haldi, food sold on the streets of Sri Lanka. We adapted this flavorful dish using familiar techniques and ingredients found in your local market. The combination of bright lime, creamy coconut milk, and fresh ginger create a tasty, kid-friendly summertime soup you will love feeding to your family.

For the soup:

½	lb raw shrimp	2	yellow onions
1	lb white fish, such as halibut, cod, or tilapia	1	quart chicken broth
¼	cup roasted cashews	1	can (15-oz) light coconut milk
3	cloves garlic	2	juicy limes
2	inch piece fresh ginger	2	tsp organic brown sugar
1	bunch cilantro, leaves and stems	2	tbsp extra virgin olive oil, divided
½	tsp crushed red pepper	3	cups cooked brown rice

For the seasonings:

1	tsp ground fennel	½	tsp sea salt
1	tsp ground coriander	½	tsp black pepper
1	tsp ground turmeric		

Moily Haldi is a delicate and complex summer soup for the whole family. Please do not omit any of the ingredients (unless you have a nut allergy). Moily Haldi is the perfect example of how Indian cooking combines heat, sweet, sour, and savory to create a perfectly balanced finished product. The flavors are sure to send your tastebuds into euphoria! Moily Haldi is naturally gluten-free. Serves four to six.

Instructions:

Prepare your ingredients: Peel and coarsely chop 3 cloves of garlic and a 2-inch piece of ginger. Dice 2 yellow onions. Separate cilantro stems from leaves and coarsely chop. Remove all produce from cutting board. If necessary, peel shrimp. Cut fish into small bite size pieces.

In a small bowl or ramekin, combine all ingredients listed under "for the seasonings".

Prepare your cashew paste: Heat a small flat skillet over medium heat for about 5 minutes. When hot, add 1 tbsp extra virgin olive oil and heat an additional 30 seconds, until oil shimmers. Add cashews, ginger, and garlic to skillet. Sauté for 2 – 3 minutes, until garlic and ginger are fragrant and cashews are lightly browned. Transfer contents of skillet to a mini food processor. Add coarsely chopped cilantro stems and ½ tsp crushed red pepper. Pulse for 2 minutes or until a thick paste has formed. Set aside.

Prepare your Moily haldi: Heat a 4-quart or larger soup pot over medium heat for about 5 minutes. When hot, add remaining tablespoon extra virgin olive oil and heat an additional 30 seconds, until oil shimmers. Add diced onion to pot and sauté for about 10 minutes, stirring occasionally until onions are soft and translucent. Add combined seasonings to onion and stir 2 minutes more, being mindful not to let the spices burn. Pour chicken broth, coconut milk, 2 tsp brown sugar, and about ½ of the cashew paste into pot. Bring mixture just to a boil. Reduce heat to medium low and simmer uncovered for 10 minutes. Add fish and shrimp, and simmer 3 minutes more. Turn off heat. Stir in ½ of the cilantro leaves and remaining cashew paste.

Getting it on the table: Place a scoop of hot brown rice into each bowl (I used an ice cream scoop). Ladle soup on top and garnish with remaining cilantro leaves. Serve and enjoy!

> Those with nut allergies can use prepared white beans instead of cashews. Vegetarians can use 3 cups prepared white beans and vegetable broth in place of the seafood and chicken broth.

The next time I make this, I want to try..._____

My actual cooking times for this recipe were..._____

I'm going to share this recipe with..._____

Black Bean and Corn Enchilada Pie

Inspired by Christina Neil

START TO FINISH: ABOUT 1 HOUR, 20 MINUTES ACTIVE

My good friend Christina is in charge of feeding two picky boys. After tasting her version of this recipe at a potluck playdate, I understand why her family requests this dish again and again. Her family is semi-vegetarian and loves that this dish can be prepared both with grass-fed ground beef and with non-GMO soy crumbles. It travels well, can be prepared up to a day ahead, and freezes beautifully! Just last week, I made a double batch of these enchilada pies on a day we were entertaining friends for Sunday supper. I prepared one 13 x 9 inch dish to serve to our guests for dinner that evening. I then divided the second batch into two disposable 8 x 8's, and stashed them in the freezer for the upcoming back-to-school shuffle this fall. When properly stored in a labeled and dated freezer bag, these enchilada pies will taste fresh for at least three months. Do remember to allow an extra 20 – 30 minutes covered baking time when prepared from frozen.

1	pound ground beef		2	tbsp chili powder
	-or-		1½	tsp garlic salt
1	pound soy crumbles		1	tsp ground cumin
½	cup diced red onion		½	tsp dried oregano
1½	cups prepared black beans (or one 14-oz can)		½	tsp sea salt
1½	cups frozen corn		½	tsp black pepper
4	oz can green chilies		2	cups shredded cheddar cheese
28	oz can tomato sauce		10	6-inch corn tortillas

This is another great kid-friendly dinner for the family on a budget. We love grass-fed ground beef. High in omega-3's and CLA's, this type of beef is even more nutritious than most fish. Stretching just one pound of ground beef to feed your family two separate dinners is also a great way to save a few dollars. When prepared using 100% corn tortillas, this dish is naturally gluten-free and nut-free. When prepared using non-GMO soy crumbles, this dish easily goes vegetarian. When serving guests, make a simple romaine salad tossed with the dressing from "Cumin-Lime Taco Salad". For just the family, serve this as a one-dish meal.

Instructions:

> **Work ahead!!!** These enchilada pies can be completely assembled up to a day ahead! Also, if you make a double batch, you will need to simmer your filling an additional 10 minutes.

Prepare your ingredients: Mince about ½ cup red onion (½ small, ¼ large). Drain and rinse black beans. Open tomato sauce and green chilies. Place ¼ to ½ cup tomato sauce on the bottom of each baking dish, just enough to cover and prevent the tortillas from sticking. In a small bowl or ramekin, combine 2 tbsp chili powder, 1 tsp ground cumin, 1½ tsp garlic salt, and ½ tsp oregano.

Prepare your pie filling: Heat a large deep skillet over medium high heat for about 5 minutes. Add ground beef to skillet and brown for 5 – 6 minutes, until no longer pink. Season with ½ tsp each sea salt and freshly ground black pepper. When meat has browned, add all remaining tomato sauce, 1½ cups frozen corn kernels, undrained green chilies, red onion, beans, and combined spices. Bring mixture just to a boil. Reduce heat to medium low and simmer for 15 minutes. Turn off heat.

Crisp your tortillas: While mixture simmers, heat a large flat skillet over medium high heat (this can also be done with a griddle or electric skillet). Working in batches, "fry" your tortillas for about one minute per side, until they start to get crispy but not burnt. Set aside. (Do not layer tortillas in skillet, they will get mushy.)

Assemble your pies: Tear tortillas in half. Use 5 tortilla halves to cover the bottom of each 8 x 8 dish (or 10 halves for one 13 x 9). Pour ¼ of the filling (just eyeball it) on top of tortillas. Cover with ½ cup cheese. Repeat with another layer of tortillas, mixture, and cheese. Cover disposable dish with aluminum foil and seal in a labeled and dated freezer bag. Cover and refrigerate tonight's dinner until ready to bake.

Getting it on the table: One hour before you want to eat dinner, preheat your oven to 350 degrees. Bake enchilada pie covered for 30 minutes. Remove foil and bake an additional 10 – 15 minutes, until cheese is hot and bubbly. Let stand 10 minutes before serving.

The next time I make this, I'm going to try..._____

My actual cooking times for this dish were..._____

I'm going to share this recipe with..._____

Chicken, Cherry, and Red Bean Curry
served over hot brown rice

START TO FINISH: 1 HOUR, 30 MINUTES ACTIVE

When cherries are in season, we use them in any way possible. This mild, but flavorful dish was created to introduce Annie to the exciting world of curry. Not only did she love it, but everyone else did as well! Our red bean and cherry curry is the perfect balance of savory and sweet, is simple to prepare, and is loaded with healing herbs and spices. If there are any leftovers, be sure to save them! As with most curries, the leftovers taste fabulous reheated the next day. This recipe makes four generous servings. If fresh cherries are unavailable, frozen cherries make a suitable substitution.

For the curry:

½	lb boneless, skinless chicken thighs	1	cup light coconut milk
2	cups prepared red beans, or one 15-ounce can	1	inch piece fresh ginger
1	cup cherries	⅓	cup chopped cilantro
1	small red onion	⅓	cup roasted cashews
3	cloves garlic	½	cup golden raisins
1	cup plain Greek yogurt	1	tbsp extra virgin olive oil
		3	cups cooked brown rice

For the seasonings:

2	tsp garam masala	½	tsp dry mustard
1	tsp ground cumin	½	tsp ground turmeric
1	tsp ground coriander	1	tsp organic sugar
½	tsp white pepper	1	tsp yellow mustard seeds
¼	tsp nutmeg		
1	tsp sea salt		

When one of my best friends asked me where we got the idea to put cherries into a curry, I really wasn't sure. We'd been experimenting with different fruit sauces, cherries are one of my favorite fruits, and well, a cherry curry just sounded tasty. All I can say is, I'm glad we did. This recipe rocks! Vegetarians can omit the chicken and double the amount of beans. Those with nut allergies can use roasted pumpkin seeds (pepitas) in place of the cashews. This dish is naturally gluten-free.

Instructions:

Prepare your ingredients: In a small bowl or ramekin, combine all ingredients listed under "for the seasonings". Dice 1 red onion. Peel and mince a 1-inch piece of ginger and 3 cloves of garlic. Pit and halve 1 cup of cherries. Coarsely chop ⅓ cup cilantro leaves and ⅓ cup cashews. Whisk together 1 cup of Greek yogurt and 1 cup of light coconut milk. After removing all produce from cutting board, dice about ½ pound of chicken thighs into ½ inch bites.

Prepare your curry: Heat a large deep skillet (or wok) over medium heat for about 5 minutes. Add 1 tbsp extra virgin olive oil and heat an additional 30 seconds, until oil shimmers. Add diced red onion and sauté for about 7 minutes, until onion is soft and translucent. Stir in minced ginger, garlic, and combined spices. Stir continuously for about 2 minutes, being mindful not to let the spices burn. (The yellow mustard seeds may begin to pop like popcorn, this is okay.) Add diced chicken breast, red beans, cherries, golden raisins, and combined Greek yogurt and coconut milk. Stir constantly until mixture comes to a boil (2 – 3 minutes). Reduce heat to medium-low and simmer uncovered for 25 minutes, stirring occasionally. Turn off heat and let curry stand for about 5 minutes.

Stock your freezer!!! Cooked brown rice is one of my favorite convenience foods. Overpaying for the precooked little pouches at the grocery store is not, especially when making your own is super easy! Whenever I make rice, I like to make a huge pot (usually 4 cups rice, 1 quart of chicken broth, and 1 quart of water). Once the cooked rice has cooled, I freeze it in 1-cup increments in small freezer bags. Whenever a recipe calls for cooked brown rice, I pull out just the amount I need. Waste not, want not, and save some green! Nice.

Pulling it all together: While curry rests, heat cooked brown rice until it is piping hot. Place hot rice in the bottom of a large serving bowl. Pour curry mixture over top. Garnish with chopped cilantro and cashews. Serve and enjoy!

The next time I make this, I'm going to try..._____

My actual cooking times for this dish were..._____

I'm going to share this recipe with..._____

Roasted Tomato and Walnut Pesto
garnished with a kalamata olive, tomato, and basil coulis

START TO FINISH: 30 MINUTES, 10 MINUTES ACTIVE

When tomato season hits its peak, we look for every way possible to utilize the bounties of our little garden. This recipe was created to throw a not-so-classic, but super tasty, comfort food into the mix. Roasting the tomatoes in a baking dish allows you to retain all of the liquid that bakes out. The virtually calorie-free "sauce" is then used as a replacement for almost all of the olive oil used in traditional pesto. This drastically cuts down on the total amount of fat and calories. The pesto can be made up to a day ahead, freezes beautifully (I use ice cube trays), and both of my girls absolutely adore it! Bon appetit!

For the pesto:

1½	cups vine ripe tomatoes	⅓	cup Parmigiano-Reggiano
6	cloves garlic	1	tbsp extra virgin olive oil
½	cup fresh basil leaves, packed snug but not stuffed	½	tsp + ½ tsp sea salt
		½	tsp + ½ tsp black pepper
⅓	cup roasted walnuts	8	- 16 oz linguini noodles

For the coulis (double if making a full box of linguini):

¾	cup chopped tomatoes, seeded	½	cup kalamata olives
		2	tbsp extra virgin olive oil
¼	cup fresh basil leaves	¼	tsp black pepper

> **Did you know?** Roasting your tomatoes greatly increases the amount of lycopene your body is able to absorb.

This recipe makes enough pesto for an entire pound of linguini. We usually prepare just ½ a box of noodles at once. We either freeze the other half of the pesto for a future dinner or use it as a dip for veggies and crackers throughout the week. If you decide to make a whole pound of pasta, you will want to double the ingredients for the coulis. This dinner is naturally vegetarian. Those sensitive to gluten can proceed as written, but use quinoa spaghetti. Those sensitive to nuts can use pepitas (roasted pumpkin seeds) in place of the walnuts. Leftovers are de-light-ful!

Instructions:

Preheat oven to 375 degrees.

While oven heats, roast your tomatoes and garlic: Coarsely chop about 1½ cups of tomatoes, trying to keep as much of the juice contained as possible. Place tomatoes in an 8 x 8 inch glass baking dish. Smash and peel 6 cloves of garlic (use the flat side of a chef's knife). Add garlic to tomatoes. Using clean hands, toss tomatoes and garlic with 1 tbsp extra virgin olive oil, and ½ tsp each sea salt and fresh ground black pepper. Transfer dish to oven, and bake for 20 minutes at 375 degrees. Remove dish from oven and let cool for about 5 minutes.

When 10 minutes remain on the tomatoes, begin heating the water for your linguini and make your coulis: While pasta water heats, coarsely chop tomatoes, kalamata olives, and fresh basil. Drizzle with 2 tbsp extra virgin olive oil and ¼ tsp black pepper. When water comes to a rolling boil, cook linguini according to package directions.

Prepare your pesto: When tomatoes and garlic have slightly cooled, transfer them to a mini food processor (or blender). Add all remaining ingredients listed under "for the pesto". Be sure to include the remaining 1/2 tsp each sea salt and fresh ground black pepper. Blend for 2 - 3 minutes, until pesto has reached a nice, creamy consistency.

Quick tip!!! Because the water content of tomatoes varies, your pesto may initially be too thick or too thin. To thin pesto, add an additional tablespoon of extra virgin olive oil. To thicken pesto, add an additional tablespoon of walnuts. Repeat until the desired consistency is met.

Pulling it all together: After draining linguini, return to pot. Toss with enough pesto to evenly coat noodles. Transfer to a serving bowl (or divide among individual bowls) and garnish with the coulis. Serve and enjoy!

The next time I make this, I'm going to try..._____

My actual cooking times for this dish were..._____

I'm going to share this recipe with..._____

Lemon-Herb Roasted Chicken
alongside a mandarin orange and mixed green salad

START TO FINISH: 1 HOUR 30 MINUTES, 20 MINUTES ACTIVE

Growing up, my mom never prepared whole chickens. In fact, the only time I ever ate chicken on the bone was when it came out of a bucket. Awhile back, I noticed that a four pound, organic chicken costs about $10.00. In order to enjoy organic chicken on our budget, we decided it was time to start roasting chicken. The first attempt was okay, but we knew we could do better. When the desired results were finally achieved, our family couldn't get enough! The meat was so tender (both white and dark) that even toothless Ellie gobbled it down. The salad is a refreshing side item for a hot summer night; flavorful tarragon paired with crunchy celery, toasted almonds and sweet oranges is sure to excite any palate.

For the chicken:

4	- 5 lb whole chicken	½	tsp sea salt
½	lemon	½	tsp fresh ground black
1	tbsp extra virgin olive oil		pepper

Handful of fresh herbs, 4 – 8 sprigs (parsley, sage, rosemary, thyme, or any combination)

For the salad:

5	cups mixed baby greens, or one 5-oz bag	2	green onions
11	oz can mandarin orange in juice (not syrup)	¼	cup toasted almonds, I prefer slivered
2	ribs celery	¼	cup gorgonzola cheese,

For the tarragon vinaigrette:

2	tbsp extra virgin olive oil	1	tsp dried tarragon
1	tbsp white wine vinegar	½	tsp sea salt
2	tsp organic sugar	½	tsp black pepper

To brine the chicken:

½	lemon	¼	cup organic sugar
¼	cup sea salt	2	- 3 quarts water

Start brining your chicken at least a day before you want to roast it. This chicken is super moist, making it very kid-friendly. Vegetarians can double the amount of almonds and cheese to make the salad a main dish. This dinner is completely gluten-free and those sensitive to nuts can simply omit the almonds.

Instructions:

About a day before you wish to roast your chicken, get the chicken brining: In a large pot with lid, dissolve ¼ cup each organic sugar and sea salt in one quart of filtered water. (Just stir until dissolved, no need to heat or anything.) Place chicken in pot. Add additional filtered water until chicken is completely covered plus one inch. Squeeze and then drop half a lemon into the pot. Cover with lid and refrigerate for 18 – 48 hours, whatever is most convenient for you.

Prepare the vinaigrette: Whisk together all ingredients listed under "for the tarragon vinaigrette". Cover and refrigerate until ready to use. This can be done up to three days ahead.

Toast your almonds: Heat a small skillet over medium heat. When hot, add almonds to skillet. Stir constantly for about 2 minutes, until almonds are lightly browned and fragrant. This can also be done up to three days ahead.

No roasting pan? No problem! Line a rimmed baking sheet with aluminum foil (to catch the drippings). Place a wire cooling rack on top of foil. Place your chicken on the cooling rack and you have a budget roasting pan! (If you want to purchase one, try to wait until November. Many stores put them on sale just before the holidays. After using a coupon and mail-in rebate, I got one for just $8.00!)

Roast your chicken: Preheat oven to 425 degrees. While oven heats, get out your roasting pan (or follow the suggestion above).   Remove chicken from brining solution and place on rack, breast side up. Squeeze half a lemon over chicken. Place squeezed lemon and fresh herbs into the cavity of the bird. Wash hands. Drizzle chicken skin with 1 tbsp extra virgin olive oil and rub into skin. Wash hands again. Season the chicken with ½ tsp each sea salt and fresh ground pepper. When oven is hot, bake for 45 – 60 minutes, or until a thermometer registers 165 degrees when inserted into the thickest part of the bird, usually the thigh. (I take the birds temperature in a few different places, just because I'm scared of undercooked chicken). Let chicken rest on rack for about 15 minutes. This will help redistribute the juices and keep your fingers from getting burned.

While the chicken rests, prepare your salad: Thinly slice 2 ribs of celery and 2 scallions. Drain 1 can of mandarin oranges. Combine with mixed greens, toasted almonds, and gorgonzola cheese. Toss with tarragon vinaigrette.

Getting it on the table: Transfer chicken to a serving platter and serve alongside the bowl of salad. Let each member of the family pick out their favorite part of the chicken. If you don't have a carving knife, don't worry. This chicken is so tender that any knife will do. Serve and enjoy!

About the portions... Because leftover salad often goes to waste, this salad provides just 3 – 4 servings. The chicken will easily serve 4 – 6, often with leftovers. If your family is larger, double the ingredients in the salad. Additionally, gorgonzola (blue) cheese pairs really well with the sweet dressing. If it is too flavorful of a cheese for your family, feta or goat cheese makes a suitable substitution.

The next time I make this, I'm going to try..._____

My actual cooking times for this dish were..._____

I'm going to share this recipe with..._____

How to make your own chicken stock...

After dinner has been served and the chicken has been picked clean, return the carcass (including the lemon and herbs) and any pan drippings to the pot that you brined it in. (This can also be done in a slow cooker.) Coarsely chop 3 carrots, 2 stalks celery, and 1 onion, peels and all. Add 1 heaping tablespoon of minced garlic (the jarred kind for simplicity), about a teaspoon of peppercorns, and a 1/2 tsp sea salt. Pour 3 quarts filtered water over the top and cover with a tight fitting lid. Let pot simmer over low heat overnight or up to 12 hours. Using a mesh strainer, strain stock into a large bowl, and refrigerate. The fat will naturally rise to the top when thoroughly chilled. Skim off fat and transfer to small jars (or quart-size freezer bags). To use, defrost in the refrigerator over night. (I freeze mine in 2 cup increments.) You can now use your homemade chicken stock in any recipe that calls for chicken broth!

Broccolini and Chicken Sausage Penne

START TO FINISH: 35 MINUTES, MOSTLY ACTIVE

Fully cooked chicken sausage is one of our go-to ingredients on nights that we need to get dinner on the table fast. It is healthy, kid-friendly, and adds a great dimension of flavor to an otherwise simple dish. (Do be sure to source brands that are made without nitrates and that use antibiotic-free chicken.) This simple dinner is a great example of how high quality ingredients come together to create a flavorful dish the whole family is sure to love. If you've never cooked with broccolini, prepare to be impressed! When properly prepared, the supermodel of broccoli (tall and skinny) is firm to the bite, packed with nutrients, and a fun way to add a bit of variety to your family's vegetable routine.

1	package fully cooked chicken sausage, four links, 12 – 16 ounces
2	cups broccolini
3	cups penne pasta, ½ standard package
1	small red onion
3	cloves garlic
10	cherry tomatoes
1	cup chicken broth
1	lemon, zest only
2	tbsp extra virgin olive oil
¼	cup Parmigiano-Reggiano cheese, plus garnish
½	tsp sea salt
½	tsp fresh ground black pepper

Yay! Another kid-friendly meal that is easy to prepare and full of healing nutrients. Feel free to use this same method with your family's favorite vegetables. Bell pepper, mushrooms, and even green beans work just as well in this tasty dish. Vegetarians can omit the chicken sausage and stir two cups of cottage cheese into the finished vegetables. Those sensitive to gluten can substitute an equal amount of brown rice penne. This dish is naturally free of nuts and any nut products. Happy eating!

Instructions:

Prepare your produce: Thinly slice 1 small red onion and 3 cloves of garlic. Cut broccolini into 2 inch pieces, approximately the same size as the penne. Slice chicken sausage on the diagonal in ½ inch slices. Halve cherry tomatoes.

Prepare your penne: In a pot of salted, boiling water, cook penne pasta according to package directions. When noodles are al dente, drain and rinse with cool water to stop the cooking process.

At the same time you begin to heat your pasta water, start your stir-fry: Heat a large, deep skillet (or wok) over medium high heat for about 5 minutes. When hot, add 2 tbsp extra virgin olive oil and heat an additional 30 seconds, until oil shimmers. Add sliced red onion and garlic to oil and sauté for about 5 minutes, until onion is tender. Season with ½ tsp each sea salt and fresh ground black pepper. Add the broccolini to skillet and sauté 3 minutes more. Finally, add the chicken sausage and brown alongside veggies for 5 minutes more. Turn heat to medium. Pour 1 cup chicken broth over veggie and sausage mixture and simmer for an additional 8 minutes. Turn off heat.

Getting it on the table: Stir halved cherry tomatoes and lemon zest into the veggie and sausage mixture. Return penne to its cooking pot and toss with contents of skillet and ¼ cup Parmigiano-Reggiano. When well combined, transfer contents of pot to a large serving bowl and garnish with a small handful of Parmigiano-Reggiano. Serve and enjoy!

Wondering what to do with your naked lemon? Use it to clean your kitchen sink! After cleaning up dinner, generously dust your sink with baking soda. Cut the naked lemon in half and use it as your "sponge". The lemon and baking soda work together to remove stains, germs, and dirt. Take that, Comet!

The next time I make this, I'm going to try..._____

My actual cooking times for this dish were..._____

I'm going to share this recipe with..._____

Simple Seared Scallops

served on a bed of triple corn polenta with goat cheese
and charred heirloom tomatoes

START TO FINISH: 40 MINUTES, 15 MINUTES ACTIVE

*Scallops just sound fancy. I suppose that is why so many of us are
afraid to prepare them at home. When a friend told me she was
teaching her high school students how to sear scallops in a foods class,
I realized the rest of us could probably do it as well. Because scallops
are on the pricier side, this meal needed to be special all the way
around. I challenged myself to create a menu plan that would "wow"
Darren, and worthy of being served in any great farm to table restaurant.
This time of year, there is nothing fresher and tastier than sweet summer
corn and heirloom tomatoes. For that reason, corn, tomatoes, and
scallops would be the base of this special dinner. To add a little
creaminess, a homemade corn broth mixes with polenta, fresh corn, and
herbs. To compliment the savory polenta and tender scallops, smoky,
charred tomatoes. This dinner is simple to prepare and huge on flavor!*

For the scallops
1½	lbs wild sea scallops	½	tsp sea salt
2	tbsp extra virgin olive oil	½	tsp black pepper

For the fresh corn and herb polenta:
2	ears sweet summer corn	1	tbsp fresh chives
1	cup dry yellow polenta	1	tsp sea salt, or to taste
3	cups filtered water	½	tsp black pepper
1	tbsp fresh tarragon		

For the tomatoes:
2	large heirloom tomatoes	¼	tsp sea salt
2	tsp extra virgin olive oil	¼	tsp black pepper

For the finish:
4	oz goat cheese	2	tbsp fresh chives

**Not only did Darren and I love this dinner, both girls did as well!
Ellie had two bowls of the polenta, and the tender scallops were
a hit too! This dinner is naturally gluten-free and nut-free.
Vegetarians can omit the scallops, enjoying the tomatoes, goat
cheese, and polenta as is. As with most seafood, all leftovers
should be consumed within two days. Serves four to six.**

Ingredients:

Prep your scallops: Use a dish towel or paper towels to gently remove excess liquid from scallops. Season dry scallops with ½ tsp sea salt and ¼ tsp fresh ground black pepper.

> **Quick tip!!!** If you have the option, always purchase dry scallops. If you are like me and buy them frozen (what can I say, I'm cheap), make sure that you are diligent about removing all excess liquid. If you don't, the skillet will get watery and your scallops won't achieve that golden brown crust that makes them shine!

Prepare your polenta: Chop 1 tbsp of fresh tarragon and 3 tbsp of fresh chives. Set aside 2 tbsp of the chives for garnish. Cut kernels off two ears of corn. (Tip: Stand corn up vertically and run your chef's knife down ¼ of the cob. Rotate cob and repeat with remaining three sides. It helps to do this in a large bowl.) Cut cobs in half and place in a large pot with a tight fitting lid. Add 4 cups of filtered water and cover. Using high heat, bring corn cobs just to a boil. Turn off heat and allow cobs to infuse water for 15 minutes (still covered). Use tongs to remove cobs. Bring corn broth back to a boil. Whisk in 1 cup of polenta and 1 tsp sea salt. Reduce heat to medium-low and simmer for about 15 minutes, whisking occasionally to prevent lumps, and to help polenta get smooth and creamy. If polenta is done before your scallops, turn heat to low and cover.

When polenta begins to simmer, start your tomatoes: Turn broiler to high. While broiler heats, remove stems from tomatoes, and cut in half vertically (or quarters if tomatoes are exceptionally large). Drizzle tomatoes with 2 tsp extra virgin olive oil, and ¼ tsp each sea salt and fresh ground black pepper. When broiler is hot, transfer tomatoes to broiler and broil for about 5 minutes.

At the same time your broiler is heating, start heating your skillet for your scallops: Heat a large flat skillet over medium high heat for about 5 minutes. When hot, add 2 tbsp extra virgin olive oil and heat for an additional 30 seconds, until oil shimmers. Place scallops in hot oil. Make sure that the oil is evenly distributed, and coating the pan under each scallop (otherwise they will stick). CAUTION: The oil may splatter when the scallops go into the pan. DO NOT have babies playing at your feet! Sear scallops for 1 minute per side. Transfer seared scallops to a dinner plate or cutting board, loosely cover with a foil tent. Let scallops rest for about 5 minutes to finish cooking.

Pulling it all together: Stir corn kernels, 1 tbsp fresh tarragon, 1 tbsp fresh chives, and ½ tsp freshly ground black pepper into polenta. When warmed through (about 2 minutes), turn off heat. Adjust seasonings if necessary. Pour polenta onto a large serving platter. Arrange charred tomatoes creatively atop polenta. Distribute scallops on top as well, placing the side with the nicest sear up. Crumble goat cheese over dish, and garnish with chives. Alternatively, divide ingredients among dinner plates (we did not do this because Darren and I eat considerably more than Annie and Ellie, and we didn't want to waste even a bite of the succulent scallops). Serve and enjoy!

The next time I make this, I want to try..._____

My actual cooking time for this dish was..._____

I'm going to share this recipe with..._____

When it comes to summer vegetables, less is often more. When you purchase your produce fresh from the farm (or farmer's market), a bit of high quality olive oil, sea salt, pepper, and a few fresh herbs is usually all that you need to add. If you are unsure of the best way to prepare your purchases, just ask the person who grew them. Over the years, many of my tricks and techniques have come directly from the wonderful people I've met at the farmer's markets. Secret confession: I never would have come up with the idea of homemade corn broth without the tip from one of my favorite farmer mamas!

Dinners for Autumn

Chicken, Goat Cheese, & Walnut Salad

Sausage & Lentil Stew

Simple Dijon Salmon
Caramelized Brussels

Chicken & Veggie
Pasta Toss

Beef Sanchos,
Spanish Brothy Beans

Broiled Chicken Thighs,
Artichokes & Tomatoes

Wagon Wheel Fiesta
Bake

Mongolion
Beef & Broccoli

Chicken, Cashew, &
Chickpea Curry

Ragin' Cajun
Louisiana Gumbo

Pumpkin Lasagna

Bacon, Corn & Shrimp
Quinoa Risotto

Goat Cheese, Chicken and Walnut Salad
with fresh fruit and mixed greens in a tarragon vinaigrette

START TO FINISH: 5 MINUTES!!!

This is the perfect salad for a cool fall day. As apples come into season, we are always looking for ways to use them. This is basically a healthy spin on the traditional Waldorf salad. The mayonnaise based dressing has been replaced with a light and flavorful tarragon vinaigrette. The best part; you'll be ready to eat in just five minutes!

For the salad:

2	cups cooked, shredded chicken	1	fuji apple
¼	cup candied walnuts	½	cup purple grapes
2	oz goat cheese (½ cup)	6	cups mixed greens, or one 5-oz bag

For the vinaigrette:

3	tbsp extra virgin olive oil	½	tsp organic sugar
1	tbsp balsamic vinegar	½	tsp sea salt
½	tsp dried tarragon	½	tsp black pepper

> Because leftover salad rarely gets eaten, this recipe feeds just our small family. If you are a larger family, feel free to double or even triple the amounts. Our girls are still anti-lettuce, so we round out their meal by tossing the other components of the salad with some cubed avocado. Vegetarians can easily substitute prepared garbanzo beans for the chicken, and those sensitive to nuts can substitute pepitas or dried cranberries. This dish is naturally gluten-free.

Whisk together all ingredients listed under "for the vinaigrette". Core and cube 1 fuji apple and halve ½ cup purple grapes. If necessary, crumble goat cheese. Toss together all ingredients listed under "for the salad". Toss the salad with vinaigrette according to your preference. Serve and enjoy!

The next time I make this, I'm going to try..._____

My actual cooking times for this dish were..._____

I'm going to share this recipe with..._____

59

Sausage and Lentil Stew
Inspired by Sarah Lima

START TO FINISH: 1 HOUR 20 MINUTES, 20 MINUTES ACTIVE

What a delicious and hearty dinner! My friend Sarah shared the idea of this recipe with me. Darren and I were looking to jazz up a basic lentil stew recipe and her base was perfect! After a first attempt that was way too spicy, we decided to use Dijon mustard, fresh thyme, and some other seasonings to brighten the flavor of the lentils. It turned out amazing! The best part; most of the ingredients are pantry staples and the method is super simple. This tasty stew makes great leftovers and it freezes beautifully! If you are feeling ambitious, you can make a double batch to stash in the freezer for a future dinner.
Serves four to six.

1½	cups lentils	1	quart chicken broth
1	pound bulk chicken sausage	1	quart filtered water
		¼	cup Dijon mustard
1	large red onion	1	tbsp chili powder
6	stalks celery	2	tsp cumin
5	carrots	1	tsp sea salt
1½	cups frozen corn kernels	1	tsp ground black pepper
6	sprigs fresh thyme	2	tbsp extra virgin olive oil
5	cloves garlic		

What a great one-dish meal for a chilly night! This stew is packed full of kid-friendly vegetables that will make you confident that you are feeding your family a healthy, healing dinner. (This is especially important as we head into cold and flu season.) Another bonus is the comforting way your house will smell while the whole thing simmers on the stove. Be sure to ladle your little one's soup a few minutes ahead of your own to give it time to cool. Vegetarians can easily substitute their favorite non-GMO soy sausage for the chicken sausage, and use vegetable broth in place of the chicken broth. This dish is naturally gluten-free and free of any nuts or nut products.

Instructions:

Prepare your produce: Peel and dice 1 large red onion and 5 cloves of garlic. Trim and thinly slice 6 stalks celery and 5 carrots. (If you have small children, first slice the carrots lengthwise to avoid a potential choking hazard.) Coarsely chop the leaves and tender stems from 2 of the thyme sprigs.

Pinching your pennies? If you are trying to stretch your family's food dollar, you may wonder how to substitute dried herbs for fresh. The general rule of thumb is to divide the quantity of fresh herbs by three. If a recipe calls for 1 tbsp of fresh herbs, you would simply replace it with 1 tsp of dried. In this dish, I would add 1 tsp of dried thyme in place of the fresh.

Start your stew: Heat a 4-quart or larger soup pot over medium-high heat for about 5 minutes. Add 2 tbsp extra virgin olive oil and heat an additional 30 seconds, until oil shimmers. Add prepared veggies (not including the thyme) and 1½ cups frozen corn kernels to pot. Season with 1 tsp each sea salt and ground black pepper and sauté for about 5 minutes. Transfer veggies to a large mixing bowl. Place sausage in now empty soup pot and sauté for about 5 minutes. When sausage is browned, return veggies to pot and pour 1 quart chicken broth, 1 quart filtered water, and 1½ cups lentils into pot. Season with ¼ cup Dijon mustard, 4 whole thyme sprigs, 1 tbsp chili powder, and 2 tsp ground cumin. Bring stew just to a boil. Reduce heat to medium low and simmer uncovered for 1 hour, stirring occasionally.

Ingredient tip: No bulk chicken sausage? No problem! Simply buy a pound of uncooked chicken sausage links and remove the casings yourself. For this dish, I prefer sweet Italian.

Getting it on the table: When hour has lapsed, turn off heat and stir in remaining chopped thyme. Ladle a generous portion of stew into each bowl. If desired, garnish with an additional sprig of thyme and serve with crusty bread. Serve and enjoy!

The next time I make this, I'm going to try..._____

My actual cooking times for this dish were..._____

I'm going to share this recipe with..._____

Simple Seared Wild Salmon
served alongside caramelized brussel sprouts

START TO FINISH: 30 MINUTES, MOSTLY ACTIVE

Many of the parents I talk to tell me that they are scared to prepare wild salmon at home. I completely understand! I used to be intimidated as well. Once Darren helped me master this simple method, I was hooked. The key to getting the crispy golden crust (that makes restaurant salmon so tasty) is to get your skillet nice and hot before you put the fish in. Also, the side of the salmon you sear first is going to be the one that is the most attractive. For the best presentation, always make sure that you sear your salmon skin side up first. If you are using salmon defrosted from the freezer, gently pat it with paper towels to remove any excess moisture. With regard to the brussel sprouts... please don't be a hater. I was for years, and am so glad that I finally came around. After being forced to try them at a restaurant I was currently working in, I realized that fresh and properly prepared brussel sprouts are delicious! Try them; you may have a new favorite vegetable!

For the salmon:

1	lb wild salmon	½	tsp sea salt
2	tbsp extra virgin olive oil	½	tsp black pepper

For the (yummy!) brussel sprouts:

1	lb brussel sprouts	1	tsp organic sugar
1	small red onion	½	tsp smoked paprika
3	cloves garlic	½	tsp dry mustard
2	slices nitrate-free bacon	⅛	tsp cayenne pepper
¼	cup grated asiago cheese	½	tsp sea salt
1	tbsp extra virgin olive oil	½	tsp black pepper
1	tbsp balsamic vinegar		Lemon wedges, to squeeze

The brussel sprouts serve four to six, and the leftovers taste fantastic. The salmon is more about the method than the amount. We consider one 6-ounce fillet to be an adult portion and one 3-ounce fillet for a small child. For one pound of salmon, you need two tablespoons olive oil and ¼ teaspoon each sea salt and black pepper. Please do the math for your family accordingly. This dish is naturally gluten-free and nut-free. Though not a complete meal, the brussel sprouts can be prepared by omitting the bacon and sautéing onion and garlic in an additional tablespoon of olive oil for vegetarians.

Instructions:

Preparations for the brussel sprouts: Trim the stems and halve brussel sprouts. Toss sprouts with 1 tbsp each extra virgin olive oil and balsamic vinegar. Set aside. Thinly slice 1 small red onion (½ large) and 3 cloves garlic. If using block cheese, grate ¼ cup asiago. Use kitchen shears or serrated knife to cut 2 slices nitrate-free bacon into ¼ inch strips.

Sauté your sprouts: Heat a large deep skillet over medium heat for about 5 minutes. When hot, add sliced bacon and sauté for about 5 minutes, until bacon is crispy. Use a slotted spoon to remove bacon crumbles from skillet. Reserve for garnish. Add sliced onions and garlic to bacon drippings and sauté for 5 minutes, stirring up any browned bacon bits in the process. Push onions and garlic to outer edges of skillet. Pour marinated brussel sprouts into center of skillet. Place lid on skillet and let rest for 4 minutes. Remove lid from skillet. Add 1 tsp organic sugar, ⅛ tsp cayenne pepper, and ½ tsp each smoked paprika, dry mustard, sea salt, and black pepper. Sauté sprouts an additional 3 minutes. Turn off heat.

While onion and garlic are sautéing, begin your salmon: Heat a large flat skillet over medium high heat for about 5 minutes. While skillet heats, season salmon with ½ tsp each sea salt and black pepper. When skillet is nice and hot, add 2 tbsp extra virgin olive oil and heat an additional 30 seconds, until oil shimmers. Place salmon fillets skin side up in hot oil and sear for 3 – 4 minutes per side, until salmon has a nice brown crust and can be removed from skillet without tearing.

Simplicity is the spice of life! Is attending to two skillets at once still a bit overwhelming? Go ahead and finish the brussel sprouts before starting the salmon. They will still be plenty warm when the salmon is ready to be served.

Pulling it all together: Toss brussel sprouts with ¼ cup asiago cheese and reserved bacon. Place a bed of brussel sprouts on each dinner plate. Top with salmon fillet, prettiest side up. If desired, serve with lemon wedges for squeezing. Serve and enjoy!

The next time I make this, I'm going to try..._____

My actual cooking times for this dish were..._____

I'm going to share this recipe with..._____

Comforting Chicken and Veggie Pasta Toss

START TO FINISH: 40 MINUTES, 20 MINUTES ACTIVE

Sometimes you just want comfort food. The original version of this recipe was created on a night that, ironically, we were both too tired to cook. I opened the fridge and was inspired by the array of classic, comforting veggies on hand. This dish is easy to throw together, very economical, and full of nutritious, healing ingredients. Our chicken and veggie pasta toss also tastes great reheated for lunch or as a quick second dinner. Serves four to six.

1	lb boneless, skinless chicken breasts	28	oz can crushed tomatoes
8	oz farfalle pasta, ½ pkg	1	cup shredded mozzarella
4	carrots	1	tbsp + 1 tsp herbs de provence
4	stalks celery	1½	tsp sea salt
1	red onion	1	tsp black pepper
5	cloves garlic	¼	cup kalamata olives
2	tbsp extra virgin olive oil	¼	cup chopped parsley, if desired
½	cup dry white wine		
½	cup chicken broth		

Do you only have cooked chicken on hand? Feel free to substitute three cups of cooked chicken for the pound of chicken breasts. Just add it with the tomato sauce. Otherwise, proceed as written!

This is one of the dinners both of my little girls absolutely love. The tender veggies are perfect for even the toothless member of your family. Vegetarians can use a pound of mushrooms in place of the chicken, and vegetable broth in place of the chicken broth. This dish can easily go gluten-free when prepared with gluten-free pasta. It is naturally free of any nuts or nut products.

Instructions:

Slicing and dicing: Peel and dice 4 carrots, 1 red onion, 5 cloves garlic, and 4 stalks celery. Remove veggies from cutting board (they can all be stored together) and cube 1 pound chicken breasts.

> For years, people were tricked into thinking that eating pasta would make them fat. That is totally untrue! When prepared using lots of healing vegetables, a light sauce, and consumed in proper portions, pasta is a great addition to a healthy diet. A generous portion of this pasta actually contains less fat and calories than many popular coffee drinks, and using 3-D shaped noodles like farfalle makes the portion appear even larger!

Prepare your Farfalle: Cook farfalle pasta one minute shy of package directions in boiling, salted water. When done boiling, drain and rinse thoroughly with cool water to stop the cooking process. Set aside.

Simultaneously, prepare your chicken and veggies: Heat a large deep skillet over medium heat for about 5 minutes. Add 3 tbsp extra virgin olive oil and heat an additional 30 seconds, until oil shimmers. Sauté mirepoix (carrots, onion, garlic, and celery) for about 10 minutes. Add diced chicken, ½ cup white wine, 1½ tsp sea salt and 1 tsp fresh ground black pepper. Sauté for 5 minutes more. Pour crushed tomatoes, herbs de Provence, and chicken broth over veggies. Increase heat to bring mixture just to a boil. Reduce heat and simmer mixture between medium low and medium heat for 15 – 20 minutes. Turn off heat.

Toss your pasta toss: Return farfalle to cooking pot. Top with 1 cup shredded mozzarella, chicken, veggies, and all remaining sauce. Use tongs to gently combine noodles with sauce and to melt cheese. Transfer to a suitably sized serving bowl and garnish with ¼ cup kalamata olives and optional parsley. Serve and enjoy!

The next time I make this, I want to try..._____

My actual cooking times for this dish were..._____

I'm going to share this recipe with..._____

Beef and Bell Pepper Sanchos
with a southwest cream sauce and Spanish brothy beans

START TO FINISH: 3 HOURS, 35 MINUTES ACTIVE

This is a creative spin on classic beef tacos that you can feel good about feeding to your family and friends. Darren taught me long ago that it is silly to waste money on taco seasoning when it is so easy to make your own. This is his "famous" seasoning blend. Feel free to double or triple the recipe. It will keep for months in a dark pantry and can be used to season tacos, quesadillas, taco salads, burritos, or any Mexican beef dish! Don't be intimidated by the beans. Cooking Spanish beans from scratch is very easy and requires little prep work. This recipe makes a large batch of beans, so I always freeze half of them (in their broth) for a future dinner side dish. Together, these two dishes are a match made in heaven (or Mexico).

For the sanchos (serves four to six):

1	lb ground beef	2	cups chopped romaine
1	red onion	1	cup chopped tomatoes
1	yellow bell pepper (or orange or red)	2	cups shredded cheddar cheese
Whole wheat tortillas		1	tbsp extra virgin olive oil

For the taco seasoning:

¼	cup ground cumin	1	tsp sea salt
1	tbsp chili powder	1	tsp black pepper
2	tsp garlic powder	½	tsp organic sugar

For the southwest cream sauce:

¼	cup sour cream	1	tsp ground cumin
2	tbsp prepared salsa	½	tsp chili powder
¼	cup chopped cilantro	¼	tsp sea salt
1	lime, zest and juice	¼	tsp black pepper

For the brothy beans (serves 12, can freeze half for future):

1	lb dry pinto beans	2	tsp Mexican oregano
6	slices nitrate-free bacon	2	tsp garlic powder
1	pint cherry or grape tomatoes	1	tsp smoked paprika
2	yellow onions	1	tsp black pepper
1	bay leaf	2	tsp sea salt
2	tsp coriander seeds	Small pinch of Spanish saffron threads	

Instructions:

Three hours or three days before you intend to eat dinner, start your brothy beans...

Preparations for the brothy beans: Dice 2 yellow onions. Halve 1 pint cherry tomatoes. In a small bowl or ramekin, combine 2 tsp coriander seeds, 2 tsp garlic powder, 2 tsp Mexican oregano, 1 tsp smoked paprika, and 1 tsp black pepper (not the sea salt). Cut 6 slices of nitrate-free bacon into ¼ inch strips.

Prepare your brothy beans: Heat a large stockpot or Dutch oven over medium heat for about five minutes. When hot, add sliced bacon. Sauté for 5 – 8 minutes, stirring occasionally, until bacon is crispy. Add diced onions and sauté 5 minutes more. Add combined seasonings to bacon. Sauté 2 minutes longer, stirring constantly and being mindful not to let the spices burn. Add 2 quarts filtered water, 1 lb dry pinto beans, halved tomatoes, bay leaf, and pinch of saffron to pot. Bring to a rolling boil and then reduce heat to a low simmer. Partially cover pot (tilt lid to allow about a 1-inch escape route for the steam) and allow beans to simmer for about 2 hours. When 2 hours have lapsed, add 2 tsp sea salt and simmer for 15 minutes more. Taste beans to make sure they are fully cooked and properly seasoned. Serve or refrigerate until ready to enjoy!

Prepare your sancho ingredients: Dice 1 onion and 1 bell pepper. Chop romaine, tomatoes, and about ¼ cup of cilantro leaves.

Prepare your taco seasoning: In a small bowl or ramekin, combine all ingredients listed under "for the taco seasoning. Set aside.

Prepare your southwest cream sauce: In a small bowl with lid, whisk together all ingredients listed under "for the southwest cream sauce." Cover and refrigerate until ready to serve.

Brown your beef: Heat a large deep skillet over medium high heat for about 5 minutes. When skillet is hot, add 1 tbsp extra virgin olive oil and heat an additional 30 seconds, until oil shimmers. Add ground beef, onion, and bell pepper to skillet. Pour combined taco seasonings over contents of skillet and sauté beef and veggies until the beef is crumbly and no longer pink. Turn off heat.

Getting it on the table: If necessary, reheat beans over medium heat until piping hot. Ladle into serving bowl. Place lettuce, tomato, cheese, beef mixture, and cream sauce into bowls alongside tortillas. Allow family members to dress their sanchos as desired. After all, isn't food always more fun is you assemble it yourself? Serve and enjoy!

Are you wondering why I call these sanchos? So did Darren. Growing up, that is what my mom called her version of soft tacos. I thought it was an everyday term. However, the first time I told Darren we were having sanchos for dinner, he looked at me like I had two heads (or at least three eyeballs). While our food got cold, we broke the "no iPhones at the table" rule to Google "sanchos". Nothing involving food came up. Next stop, Wikipedia. According to Wikipedia, "Sancho Panza is a fictional character in the novel Don Quixote written by Don Miguel de Cervantes Saavedra in 1602. Sancho acts as a squire to Don Quixote, and provides comments throughout the novel, known as sanchismos, that are a combination of broad humor, ironic Spanish proverbs, and earthy wit." Still perplexed, we called my mom to ask her why she called these sanchos. Her reply, "That it is what the greasy Mexican restaurant down the road called them." So, there's that. You got a little literary lesson along with a brief glimpse into my past.

What a great way to get your kids to eat more veggies!!! Anything they can assemble themselves, eat with their hands, and top with sauce is sure to be a winner. Vegetarians can substitute two tablespoons butter for the bacon in the beans, and use their favorite non-GMO crumbles in place of the beef. When served with gluten-free tortillas, this meal is naturally gluten-free. It is also naturally free of any nut or nut products.

The next time I make this, I want to try..._____

My actual cooking times for this dish were..._____

I'm going to share this recipe with..._____

To Freeze or Not To Freeze...

Darren is not a big fan of eating leftovers. To be completely honest, neither am I. However, I do love feeding my family a cost effective made-from-scratch dinner that involves minimal time in the kitchen. By now, you already know that I am a huge fan of making an 8 x 8 today and an 8 x 8 to save. The following ideas are a few more of the things that surprise my friends when they peak inside my freezer.

Leftover cooked meat: Roasted chicken, pot roast, and pork all freeze beautifully. After dinner is over, shred any remaining meat. You can either freeze the meat as is or pour in any accompanying juices. As a reference, about 3 cups of cooked meat equals 1 pound. I freeze mine in 1½ cup (half pound) increments, and use it in any recipe calling for cooked chicken, beef, or pork.

Prepared beans: After making the switch from canned beans to dried, I had to do a little experimenting to figure out the best way to freeze them. I've discovered that it works best to freeze them in their cooking liquid. I make an entire bag of dried beans at a time and then freeze them in 1½ cup increments, adding just enough cooking liquid to cover. (1½ cups is the equivalent to one 15-oz can of canned beans.)

Cooked brown rice: Same as beans, I make a large batch at once and freeze the rice in 1-cup portions. I love that I always have a healthy whole grain on hand.

Soups, stews, chilis, and gumbos: Whenever I take the time to make a tasty but time consuming dinner, I make enough to freeze for the future. To save freezer space, I ladle the leftovers into a gallon size freezer bag and then lay it flat on the bottom shelf of my freezer. This allows me to keep a dozen soups or stews on hand using minimal space. (This is also how I freeze stocks and broths.)

Sauces: Pesto, tomato sauce, chipotle in adobo, and coconut milk can all be frozen in one tablespoon increments in an ice cube tray. Once frozen, transfer to a labeled and dated freezer bag. As a reference, 4 tbsp = ¼ cup. 3 tsp = 1 tbsp.

Broiled Chicken Thighs and Artichokes

with blistered tomatoes on a bed of lemon-parmesan couscous

START TO FINISH: 20 MINUTES, MOSTLY ACTIVE.

For years, we completely ignored the broiler function on our oven. Then we realized how quickly it could turn simple ingredients into a quick, easy, and healthy meal. Now, we are hooked. Broiling the chicken thighs gets dinner on the table fast, gives the chicken a nice char, and keeps the meat nice and moist. Using marinated artichokes adds a great flavor with virtually no effort, and the lemon-parmesan couscous takes just minutes to prepare. When I did the final test on this recipe, Darren said, "You know? I always really enjoy this dinner". Annie and Ellie ate as much chicken as we did! Winner, winner, chicken dinner. Serves four to six.

For the chicken and veggies:

1½	lbs boneless, skinless chicken thighs	1	tbsp extra virgin olive oil
2	cups marinated artichokes	½	tsp sea salt
1	cup cherry tomatoes	½	tsp black pepper

For the lemon-parmesan couscous:

1⅓	cups whole wheat couscous	2	tbsp extra virgin olive oil
1⅓	cups chicken broth		
½	cup Parmigiano-Reggiano	½	tsp sea salt
½	cup flat leaf parsley, chopped fine	½	tsp black pepper
1	lemon, zest and juice		

I love serving my girls dark meat chicken. It is higher in iron and many B vitamins than the white counterpart, costs about $2.00 less per pound, and is still lower in fat than beef. It also stays super moist when cooked; this makes it a perfect first animal protein for babies. The iron will help prevent anemia and the B vitamins will aid in your little one's brain development. Vegetarians can omit the chicken thighs, double the amount of vegetables and cheese, and cook the couscous in vegetable broth instead of chicken broth. Those sensitive to gluten can use quinoa instead of the couscous, adjusting cooking times and amount of broth as necessary (double check the ingredients on the artichokes). This dish is naturally nut-free.

Instructions:

Preheat broiler.

While broiler heats, prepare your ingredients: Drain artichokes and finely chop ½ cup flat leaf parsley. Drizzle 1 tbsp extra virgin olive oil over chicken thighs, and season with ½ tsp each sea salt and black pepper. Place chicken thighs on broiler pan and broil for 6 minutes. Turn chicken thighs and add artichokes and tomatoes to broiler pan. Broil 6 – 8 minutes more, until chicken thighs reach an internal temperature of 165 degrees.

> **Ingredient tip!** When purchasing marinated artichokes, be sure to source brands that use extra virgin olive oil. Otherwise, you could be exposing your family to genetically modified vegetable or canola oils. When you drain your artichokes, do not rinse them. The flavor in the remaining oil is part of what makes this simple dinner so tasty.

When your chicken goes into the broiler, start your couscous: Bring 1⅓ cups chicken broth just to a boil. Remove from heat, stir in 1⅓ cups couscous, and cover with a tight fitting lid. After 5 minutes, fluff couscous with a fork. Once couscous has been fluffed, stir in Parmigiano-Reggiano, lemon zest and juice, chopped parsley, 2 tbsp extra virgin olive oil, and ½ tsp each sea salt and black pepper.

Pulling it all together: Place a bed of couscous on each plate. Top with divided chicken thighs, artichokes, and tomatoes. If desired, garnish with additional parsley. Serve and enjoy!

> **Serving couscous to toddlers:** Does your toddler still struggle with the spoon? So do mine! When Annie first started feeding herself, we started stirring plain yogurt into her couscous. She was able to get the couscous to her mouth on her own, and I didn't have to spend an extra 20 minutes cleaning up the mess!

The next time I make this, I want to try..._____

My actual cooking times for this dish were..._____

I'm going to share this recipe with..._____

Wagon Wheel Fiesta Bake

START TO FINISH: 20 MINUTES TO ASSEMBLE, PLUS BAKE TIME.

This is officially Annie's first "recipe". On a recent grocery trip, Annie grabbed a bag of wagon wheels (of course they put them right at her eye level), handed them to me, and (in her most serious tone) said, "Mommy, I want this to dinner today". I looked her in the eye and said, "Okay Annie, what would you like to eat them with?" You could tell the wheels were turning as she tapped her chin and said, "Let me think." (Pause, pause, pause.) "Oh, I know! Tomatoes! Oh, and chicken!" I've got to tell you, I was so impressed and proud! (Hence the fact that I am bragging about it here.) I told her that sounded delicious and to put the noodles in the cart. I spent all of that afternoon's naptime creating a southwest mac and cheese recipe that I knew everyone would love. She loved it, we loved it, and I'm sure that your family will love it too!

For the fiesta bake:

1	lb wagon wheel shaped pasta		1	tbsp butter
1	pound cooked, shredded chicken (about 3 cups)		3	tbsp white whole wheat flour
1	pint cherry tomatoes		3	cups whole milk
1	large onion, any color		1	cup shredded mozzarella cheese
2	tbsp extra virgin olive oil		4	oz cream cheese

Seasonings for the fiesta bake:

1	tbsp powdered mustard		½	tsp ground nutmeg
1	tbsp ground cumin		¼	tsp cayenne
1	tbsp smoked paprika		1	tsp sea salt
2	tsp garlic powder		1	tsp black pepper

For the cheesy, crunchy topping:

1	cup whole wheat panko breadcrumbs		½	tsp sea salt
1	cup shredded mozzarella		½	tsp black pepper
¼	cup Parmigiano-Reggiano		1	tbsp extra virgin olive oil

This is another one of those amazing recipes that not only can be assembled up to a day ahead, it makes enough to feed a familiy of four to six twice! An 8 x 8 for dinner tonight, an 8 x 8 to freeze. It is also super kid-friendly and the leftovers taste great!

Instructions:

Prepare your ingredients: Dice 1 onion. Halve 1 pint cherry tomatoes. In a small bowl or ramekin, combine all ingredients listed under "seasonings for the fiesta bake". Set aside. In a small mixing bowl, combine all ingredients listed under "for the cheesy, crunchy topping".

Cook your wagon wheels: In a pot of salted boiling water, cook wagon wheels one minute shy of package directions. Drain and immediately rinse with cool water to stop the cooking process. Drain again.

When you begin heating the water for the pasta, start your roux: Heat a large saucepan over medium heat for about 5 minutes. When saucepan is hot, add 2 tbsp butter, 1 tbsp extra virgin olive oil, and 3 tbsp white whole wheat flour (or whatever you have on hand). Whisk constantly for 5 minutes, being mindful not to let the roux burn. Add 3 cups whole milk, onion, and combined seasonings to roux. Once mixture comes just to a boil, reduce heat to medium low and simmer for 10 minutes. When 10 minutes have lapsed, whisk 1 cup shredded mozzarella and ¼ cup Parmigiano-Reggiano into sauce. When melted, turn off heat.

Pulling it all together: Stir chicken, cooked wagon wheels, and tomatoes into cheese sauce. Pour half of the fiesta bake into each 8 x 8 inch baking dish (or one 13 x 9). Top each dish with half of the topping. Cover tonight's dinner with plastic wrap and refrigerate until ready to bake. Cover the disposable dish with foil, place in a labeled and dated freezer bag, and freeze for a future dinner.

Baking instructions: If baking immediately after assembling, bake uncovered for 30 minutes. If baking from the fridge, bake uncovered 40 – 50 minutes. If baking from the freezer, bake covered for 1 hour. Remove foil and bake an additional 15 minutes, until topping is nice and crunchy.

Modifications: This dish can easily go vegetarian by simply omitting the chicken. It is naturally nut-free. Those sensitive to gluten can use brown rice flour in place of the wheat flour and brown rice fusilli in place of the wagon wheels. Happy eating!

The next time I make this, I want to try..._____

My actual cooking times for this dish were..._____

I'm going to share this recipe with..._____

Mongolion Beef and Broccoli

START TO FINISH: 30 MINUTES, MOSTLY ACTIVE.

We love to recreate popular restaurant dishes at home. "Mongolion Beef" and "Stir-fried Beef and Broccoli" are classics offered at Chinese restaurants nationwide. We decided to combine the two to create a healthified, lower sugar, lower fat version of these popular dinners. Instead of flash frying the beef (as most Chinese restaurants do), it is browned in just a small amount of sesame and olive oil. This not only works great, it is super tasty as well! If you like your Chinese with a little heat, I highly recommend serving this dish with Sriracha hot chili sauce. It really kicks it up a notch!

For the stir-fry:

1	lb sirloin steak	1	tbsp extra virgin olive oil
3	cups broccoli florets		
2	tbsp sesame seeds	2	tbsp cornstarch
1	tbsp sesame oil	3	cups cooked brown rice

For the Mongolion stir-fry sauce:

2	tbsp hoisin sauce	¼	cup chicken broth
1	tbsp mushroom flavored (or dark) soy sauce	1	tsp organic brown sugar
		1	tbsp rice vinegar
1	inch piece ginger	½	tsp crushed red pepper
2	green onions		

Hoisin sauce is a sweet and spicy soy-based sauce that is often used in traditional Asian cooking. It is available in the Asian section of most large grocery store chains, Asian markets, or online. When purchasing hoisin sauce, please be sure to read the ingredients. Some brands try to sneak in red no. 40 or high fructose corn syrup.

This recipe is packed with flavor, but still mild enough to appeal to toddlers. I think that this was the first time Ellie actually ate steak. Feel free to double the amount of crushed red pepper if you are daring! Vegetarians can easily substitute organic extra firm tofu for the steak, and use vegetable broth in place of the chicken broth. Those sensitive to gluten need to simply source gluten-free hoisin sauce and soy sauce (supposedly Kake brand is, but please double check. This dish is naturally nut-free. Serves four to six.

Preparations:

All preparations can be done up to a day ahead, takes about 15 minutes.

Peel and mince a 1-inch piece of ginger and 2 green onions.

Blanch your broccoli: Fill a large mixing bowl with ice water. Cut 3 cups of broccoli florets (from about 2 stems) into bite-size pieces. Discard stems or reserve for future use. In a large pot with steamer insert, bring 1 inch of water just to a boil. Place broccoli florets into steamer basket and steam for about a minute, just until the broccoli takes on a bright, green color. Immediately submit broccoli florets into ice water bath to stop the cooking process. When thoroughly cool, drain and transfer to the refrigerator until ready to use.

In a small bowl or mixing cup, combine all ingredients listed under "for the Mongolion stir-fry sauce". Whisk to dissolve sugar and thoroughly combine. Cover and refrigerate until ready to use.

Slice your steak: Use a serrated knife (tomato knife) to thinly slice steak into ¼ - ½ inch slices. Place the sliced steak and 2 tbsp cornstarch (non-GMO) in a gallon size storage bag. Seal bag and shake until steak is thoroughly coated.

> **"It's shake 'n bake, and I helped!"** Do you remember those commercials? The marketing team behind those ads were definitely on to something. Studies have repeatedly shown that kids are much more likely to try a new food when they get to help in the preparation. Once you seal the bag, let your toddler or preschooler shake up the steak. This is an easy and mess free way to let them "help" you with dinner. Annie also loves to "help" me whisk together sauces, dressings, and marinades. As long as there are no sharp knives or raw meat involved, we are always looking for ways to get her (and even little Ellie) involved in the kitchen!

Instructions:

Toast your sesame seeds: Heat a large, flat skillet over medium high heat for about 5 minutes. Add 2 tbsp sesame seeds to hot dry skillet, and stir constantly for 2 minutes, until seeds are fragrant and beginning to brown. Transfer sesame seeds to a small bowl or ramekin.

Start your stir-fry: Pour 1 tbsp each sesame oil and extra virgin olive oil into the now empty skillet. Allow oil to heat for about 30 seconds, until it shimmers. Arrange sliced steak in a single layer in the skillet (this is why we are using a large flat skillet instead of the large deep skillet or wok most stir-fries call for). Sear steak for 1 to 2 minutes per side, or until it can be turned without tearing. Add broccoli to skillet and stir-fry 1 minute more. Give stir-fry sauce a quick stir (to reincorporate ingredients), and pour in to skillet. Continue to stir-fry all ingredients until sauce has thickened and dish is hot throughout. Remove from heat.

Pulling it all together: While stir-frying steak and veggies, heat cooked brown rice until piping hot. Place hot brown rice in bottom of a serving bowl. Pour contents of skillet over rice and garnish with sesame seeds. If desired, serve with Sriracha hot chili sauce. Serve and enjoy!

The next time I make this, I'm going to try..._____

My actual cooking times for this dish were..._____

I'm going to share this recipe with..._____

Why you should not be intimidated...

Parents often tell me that they would cook more ethnic cuisine if they weren't so overwhelmed and intimidated. I hope that this cookbook will help you overcome that fear.
I personally invited myself into the homes of the amazingly diverse group of woman I am blessed to know. I watched them cook the meals of their heritage; taking notes, taking tastes, and asking questions along the way. I now hope to share that knowledge with you. Once you start making Chinese, Indian, and Spanish cuisine, the confidence will come. Remember, I was in your shoes just a few years ago! I have worked incredibly hard to make sure that the instructions presented in this book are explained in a way that even the most novice cook can understand. If something ever seems unclear to you, please do not hesitate to ask for help. As you know, you can find me on Facebook, Twitter, and HealthnutFoodie.com. If there is anything I can do to help build your confidence in the kitchen, all you have to do is ask!

Chicken, Cashew, and Chickpea Curry
Inspired by Sonal Rastogi

START TO FINISH: 1 HOUR, 30 MINUTES ACTIVE.

The spices used in Indian cooking have some amazing, healing benefits. Turmeric, the spice that gives curry its bright yellow color, has been used to fight cancer, cystic fibrosis, arthritis, and fibromyalgia. It can also decrease chronic pain and is a natural immunity booster. So often, we make the same things over and over because we are scared to reach out of our cooking "comfort box". We really should be taking advantage of the variety of cuisine available throughout the world (and not just by ordering take-out). A while back, I decided to challenge myself to come up with an easy, healthy, and delicious curry. It took a few tries, but I did it! Ladled over a bowl of hot brown rice, this dish is an amazing and impressive one-dish meal to feed your family and friends.

For the curry:

- ½ lb boneless, skinless chicken breasts
- 1½ cups prepared garbanzo beans (or one 15-oz can)
- 4 plum tomatoes
- 1 onion, any color
- 3 cloves garlic
- 1 inch piece fresh ginger
- 1 cup light coconut milk
- 1 cup Greek yogurt
- 1 tbsp extra virgin olive oil
- ⅓ cup cilantro leaves
- ⅓ cup roasted cashews
- 3 cups cooked brown rice

For the seasonings:

- 2 tsp mild curry powder
- ½ tsp ground turmeric
- ½ tsp smoked paprika
- ½ tsp ground cumin
- ½ tsp ground coriander
- ½ tsp ground cayenne
- ¼ tsp cinnamon
- 1 tsp sea salt
- ½ tsp black pepper
- 1 tsp yellow mustard seeds

This is a kid-friendly meal that you will feel proud feeding your family and friends. Greek yogurt is full of probiotics (which promotes a healthy digestive tract), and coconut milk is getting tons of press lately for being the next big thing in keeping skin supple as we age (we all know we're not getting any younger). Vegetarians can easily omit the chicken and double the amount of beans. Those with nut allergies can simply omit the cashews. This dish is naturally gluten-free.

Instructions:

Prepare the spices: Measure out all ingredients listed under "for the seasonings" and place in a small bowl or ramekin. Stir to combine and take a whiff. This will get you super excited about dinner! Set aside (if you can).

Prepare your ingredients: Dice 1 red onion. Peel and mince 3 cloves garlic and a 1-inch piece of ginger. Quarter 4 plum tomatoes. Coarsely chop ⅓ cup cilantro and ⅓ cup roasted cashews. Remove all vegetables from cutting board. Use kitchen shears (I've found this to be the easiest way) to cut ½ pound of chicken into ½ - 1 inch cubes. Wash hands thoroughly.

Prepare your curry: Heat a large, deep skillet over medium heat for about 5 minutes. Add 1 tbsp extra virgin olive oil and heat an additional 30 seconds, until oil shimmers. Add diced onion and sauté for 5 - 7 minutes, until nice and tender. Add minced garlic, ginger, and combined spices to skillet. Stir continuously for 2 minutes, being mindful not to let the spices burn. The yellow mustard seeds may begin to pop like popcorn, this is fine. Add tomatoes, chickpeas, chicken, and 1 cup each coconut milk and Greek yogurt to skillet. Stir constantly until mixture comes just to a boil (2 - 3 minutes). Reduce heat to medium low and simmer uncovered for 25 minutes, stirring occasionally.

Getting it on the table: When curry has almost finished simmering, heat your cooked brown rice until it is piping hot. Place rice in the bottom of a large serving bowl. Pour curry mixture on top. Garnish with chopped cashews and cilantro. Serve and enjoy!

Can you believe how easy and inexpensive it is to make curry from scratch?!? Feeding a family of four on just half a pound of chicken is a great way to stretch your family's food dollar. Feel free to play around with the ingredients here. Cubed pork, spinach, mushrooms, peas and carrots can all work equally well with this sauce and seasoning combination.

The next time I make this, I'm going to try..._____

My actual cooking times for this dish were..._____

I'm going to share this recipe with..._____

Ragin' Cajun Louisiana Gumbo

START TO FINISH: 4 HOURS, 1 HOUR ACTIVE.

Looking back on all of the cities we've called home, none can match the hospitality offered to us by the people of New Orleans. What you and I call parties is simply the way life is lived in the Big Easy. The gatherings are large, the food amazing, and the drinks flowing. No matter where you go or what time of day, gumbo is always on the menu. When we celebrated with different families, we realized they all had their own unique family recipe. When pressed on how to make it, everyone always replied, "Oh, it is so easy! You just make a dark roux and throw a bunch of stuff into a pot." Well, being a girl from the Midwest (who at the time had very few kitchen skills), that did not sound "so easy". I finally convinced my good friend Shawn to show me how to make truly authentic Cajun gumbo. While it does take a while to get the roux nice and dark, it is well worth the effort, and really quite simple after all!

For the gumbo:

1½	lbs boneless skinless chicken breast	10	cups chicken broth
1½	lbs uncured andouille chicken sausage	3	bay leaves
1	lb peeled, uncooked shrimp, optional	½	cup + 2 tbsp extra virgin olive oil
3	bell peppers, any color	½	cup butter
1	bunch of celery	1	cup unbleached all purpose flour
3	yellow onions	1	tbsp Worcestershire sauce
1	lb frozen okra	1	lb brown basmati rice

For the seasonings:

1	tbsp Hungarian (sweet) paprika	1½	tsp black pepper
1	tbsp garlic powder	1½	tsp dried thyme
1	tbsp sea salt	1½	tsp dried oregano
		½	tsp cayenne pepper

Garnishments:
Sliced green onions
Frank's hot sauce (or your family's favorite)

As I'm sure you realized from the ingredient list, this makes a huge pot of gumbo (12 – 16 servings). If so much effort goes into preparing the roux, we surely deserve to get multiple meals out of

it! Both the gumbo and the rice freeze beautifully (separately, of course), and it tastes great as leftovers. One pot feeds our family four separate meals! Gumbo is super kid-friendly, and Annie actually asks for "okra soup" by name! During Lenten season, this dish often goes vegetarian by simply omitting the meat, reducing the broth by two cups, and using vegetable broth in place of the chicken broth. Those sensitive to gluten can make their roux using rice flour in place of the all purpose flour; otherwise, proceed as written. This dish is naturally free of nuts or any nut products.

Instructions:

Slicing and dicing: Dice bell pepper, onion, and celery (the "holy trinity"). Remove from cutting board. Dice chicken and sausage into bite sized pieces.

Prepare your seasonings: In a small bowl or ramekin, combine all ingredients listed under "for the seasonings".

Brown your meat: Heat a large flat skillet over medium high heat for about 5 minutes. Add 2 tbsp extra virgin olive oil and heat an additional 30 seconds, until oil shimmers. Brown chicken for about 3 minutes per side. Remove chicken from skillet and brown sausages for an additional 3 – 5 minutes. Set chicken and sausage aside.

Prepare your roux: In your largest stockpot (at least 6 quarts), melt ½ cup butter and ½ cup extra virgin olive oil over medium-low to medium heat. (If you are new to roux, go with medium-low. It will take a little longer, but you will be less likely to burn your roux. If you do burn your roux, THROW IT AWAY and start over. Otherwise, you will ruin the rest of your gumbo!). When butter has melted, stir in 1 cup of unbleached all purpose flour. Using a wooden spoon, stir your roux continuously for the next 30 – 40 minutes. You want your roux to become the color of milk chocolate or a rich caramel.

Make your gumbo: When roux is ready, add the holy trinity and combined seasonings. Sauté for about 15 minutes, stirring often, until vegetables are nice and tender. Add 10 cups (2 quarts + 2 cups) chicken broth, chicken, chicken sausage, frozen okra, 3 bay leaves, and 1 tbsp Worcestershire sauce. Increase heat to bring just to a boil. Reduce heat back to medium-low and simmer uncovered for 2 ½ to 3 ½ hours.

Pulling it all together: If necessary, begin cooking your brown basmati rice one hour before you intend to enjoy dinner. Just before serving, thinly slice green onions. Ladle gumbo into bowls. Use an ice cream scoop to dish out rice. Place one scoop of rice into center of each bowl of gumbo. Garnish with a sprinkling of green onion and pass Frank's hot sauce at the table. Serve and enjoy!

Ingredient tip! Because we don't go through brown basmati rice as fast as other varieties, I like to buy just the amount we need from the bulk bin. If brown basmati rice is not available in your market, any long grain brown rice will do. Also, please note that 1 pound of bulk rice is equal to 2¼ cups of uncooked rice. When storing any type of uncooked rice, you will maximize shelf life by keeping it in the refrigerator. Cooked brown basmati rice also freezes beautifully, so feel free to make a large enough batch for all of the gumbo.

The next time I make this, I'm going to try..._____

My actual cooking times for this dish were..._____

I'm going to share this recipe with..._____

Cooking with Okra

Okra is a great nutrient packed vegetable that both of my girls really enjoy. It is also a natural thickening agent, making this gumbo taste much richer than it is. I've chosen to use frozen okra in place of fresh to considerably cut down on prep time. After being trimmed and sliced, fresh okra needs to be sautéed for about 10 minutes to cook off the "sliminess". Frozen okra does not. If you grow fresh okra or just prefer to use fresh, please do! Just make sure that you give them a good saute in a separate skillet before adding them to the rest of your gumbo.

Pumpkin Lasagna!
Loaded with Italian sausage and four types of cheese

START TO FINISH: 90 MINUTES, 30 MINUTES ACTIVE.

As the holidays approach, everyone needs an ace in their pocket when it comes to recipes. This is your ace. Whether you are entertaining friends, feeding houseguests, or responsible for contributing to a potluck, this is a dish that will wow even the most sophisticated palate. It can be assembled up to a day ahead, freezes beautifully, and is even relatively inexpensive! If you are entertaining a crowd, assemble the lasagna in a 13 x 9 inch dish. If your gathering is smaller, divide the ingredients among two 8 x 8 inch dishes. You can then stash the other one in the freezer for a last minute emergency (or when your friend has a baby). Each 8 x 8 serves six to eight.

2	lbs sweet Italian sausage	1	tsp dried thyme
1	red onion	½	tsp sea salt
4	cloves garlic	½	tsp black pepper
⅔	cup gorgonzola cheese		

2	cups pureed roasted pumpkin, or one can	1	cup shredded mozzarella cheese
1	cup ricotta cheese	½	cup Parmigiano-Reggiano cheese
2	eggs		
½	tsp ground nutmeg		

1	jar of your favorite tomato pasta sauce, 24 – 25 oz	15	oz can tomato sauce

¼	cup fresh sage leaves	2	tbsp Parmigiano-Reggiano cheese
1	cup shredded mozzarella cheese	¼	tsp black pepper
12	no-bake lasagna noodles		

This is a great meal your whole family is sure to love. For the best fusion of flavors, look for sausage that contains fennel seeds. Vegetarians can use their favorite non-GMO veggie crumbles, adding 2 tbsp of fennel seeds when browning it. Those sensitive to gluten can proceed as written when using brown rice no-bake lasagna noodles (amazon.com). This dish is naturally free of any nuts or nut products.

Instructions:

Preparations: Dice 1 red onion and 4 cloves garlic. Set aside. Stir together 1 jar of your favorite pasta sauce with 1 can of tomato sauce. Set aside. In a large mixing bowl, whisk 2 eggs. Add 2 cups pureed pumpkin and 1 cup ricotta cheese to the eggs. When well combined, stir in 1 cup shredded mozzarella, ½ cup Parmigiano-Reggiano, and ½ tsp nutmeg.

> **Did you know?** Instructions on how to roast your own pumpkin can be found on the Healthnut Foodie website!

Brown your sausage: Heat a large deep skillet over medium high heat for about five minutes. When hot, add 1 tbsp extra virgin olive oil and heat an additional 30 seconds, until oil shimmers. Add sausage, onion, and garlic to skillet. Season with 1 tsp dried thyme, and ½ tsp each sea salt and fresh ground black pepper. Stir and brown sausage for 5 – 7 minutes, breaking sausage into crumbles as it cooks. When sausage is no longer pink, turn off heat. Stir in ⅔ cups gorgonzola cheese just until melted.

Assemble your lasagna(s): Pour ¼ - ½ cup tomato sauce on the bottom of each baking dish. Place 2 no-bake lasagna noodles on the bottom of each 8 x 8. Add ¼ of the sausage mixture (eyeball it), ¼ of the pumpkin and cheese mixture, and ¼ of the sauce to each dish. Repeat with another layer of noodles, sausage, pumpkin and cheese, and sauce. Add one more layer of noodles, and then top each dish with an additional ½ cup mozzarella, 2 tbsp torn sage leaves, 2 tbsp Parmigiano-Reggiano, and ¼ tsp black pepper. Cover tonight's dinner with foil and refrigerate. Transfer disposable 8 x 8 to a labeled and dated freezer bag, and freeze. (If making just one 13 x 9, please double the amounts used in each layer.)

To bake your lasagna: One hour before you want to enjoy dinner, preheat oven to 350 degrees. When oven is hot, place foil covered lasagna in oven and bake for 45 minutes. Remove foil and bake for an additional 10 minutes, until cheese is hot and bubbly. Let lasagna rest for 5 – 10 minutes. Serve and enjoy! (If baking from frozen, please add an additional 30 – 45 minutes covered bake time.)

The next time I make this, I'm going to try..._____

My actual cooking times for this dish were..._____

I'm going to share this recipe with..._____

Bacon, Corn, and Shrimp Risotto
...starring Quinoa!

START TO FINISH: 30 MINUTES, ALL ACTIVE

This recipe took a while to perfect. Darren and I loved the initial flavor (and the nutrient profile is hard to beat), but our first attempt was missing that special something. After much contemplation, we realized we forgot to add any fat! Fat is a key component to properly balanced flavors and is one of the main reasons the fat-free versions of your favorite foods often fail. When we started to talk about the natural complements to shrimp and corn, we realized this dish needed bacon. It was a-may-zing! Who knew crazy quinoa could taste so good? The beauty of bacon is that a little goes a long way, just 3 slices of the nitrate-free variety was enough to take this recipe from good to great (while still keeping the total amount of fat at a healthy level). Because leftover seafood quickly spoils, I wrote this recipe to be just enough for two adults and two small children. If your family is larger or you are entertaining friends, double or even triple the recipe.

For the risotto:

½	pound uncooked peeled shrimp		1	red bell pepper
3	slices nitrate-free bacon		1	lime, zest and juice
1	cup uncooked quinoa		2½	cups chicken broth
1	cup frozen corn kernels		6	chives, to garnish

For the seasonings:

1	tsp garlic powder		¼	tsp red pepper flakes
1	tsp ground cumin		½	tsp sea salt
1	tsp chili powder		¼	tsp black pepper

If you've never cooked with quinoa, you are missing out! Quinoa (KEEN-wa) is an ancient "grain" that has recently been rediscovered, and is now considered one of the top "superfoods". After doing further research, I discovered that quinoa is actually not a grain at all. It is technically an edible seed, and a member of the chenopod family (the same one as spinach). In ancient times, the Incas fed quinoa to their soldiers before battle to give them the added stamina they needed to fight their enemies.

Instructions:

Preparations: Seed, core, and chop 1 red bell pepper. In a small bowl or ramekin, combine all ingredients listed under, "for the seasonings". In another small bowl or ramekin, zest and juice 1 lime. Remove all vegetables from cutting board. Use kitchen shears to cut 3 slices of nitrate free bacon into ¼ inch strips. Hand wash shears as you will need them for the chive garnish.

Brown your bacon: Heat a large deep skillet over medium heat for about 5 minutes. Add bacon to skillet and cook until crispy, 5 – 8 minutes. Use a slotted spoon to transfer bacon crumbles to a paper-towel lined plate. Do not discard bacon drippings.

Start your risotto: Add 1 cup dry quinoa and combined seasonings to bacon drippings. Stir constantly for about 2 minutes, being mindful not to let the spices burn. Reduce heat to medium low. Add ½ cup chicken broth and stir constantly until nearly all the liquid has been absorbed. Repeat four more times with remaining 2 cups broth (1/2 cup at a time). The amount of time that it takes for the quinoa to absorb the broth will continue to lengthen as the risotto progresses (about 20 – 25 minutes total). Once the quinoa have "popped" (the seed separates and it appears as though there is a ring around it, think Saturn), add ½ pound peeled and deveined shrimp. Stir 2 minutes more, just until shrimp have turned pink.

Getting it on the table: Add chopped bell peppers, corn kernels, and lime zest/juice to risotto. Continue stirring for another minute or two, until veggies are heated throughout and the risotto has reached a nice, creamy consistency. Transfer to a serving bowl. Garnish with crispy bacon and freshly snipped chives (kitchen shears work best). Serve and enjoy!

> This dish is naturally gluten-free and nut-free. It is kid-friendly as well. (I do cut the girls' shrimp into thirds.) Vegetarians can use 2 tbsp of butter in place of the bacon, vegetable broth for the chicken broth, and omit the shrimp.

The next time I make this, I'm going to try..._____

My actual cooking times for this dish were..._____

I'm going to share this recipe with..._____

Dinners for Winter

Shrimp and Soba
Stir-Fry

Popeye Manicotti
p.90

Moroccan Sausage and
Vegetable Couscous

Salsa Verde
Chicken Enchiladas
p.94

Beef and Vegetable
Chinese Noodles
p.96

Braised Chicken,
Fennel and Tomatoes
p.98

Cheesy Spinach and
Mushroom Noodle Bake
p.100

Pozole Rojo
p.102

Santa Fe
Chicken Salad
p.105

Company's Coming
Pot Roast Dinner
p.106

Maple-Mustard Chicken
Lemon-Spinach Linguinie
p.108

White Chicken Chili

Shrimp and Soba Stir-Fry

START TO FINISH: 20 MINUTES, MOSTLY ACTIVE

This meal was originally created on a beautiful spring evening. When laying out the cookbook, we realized that this was a perfect dinner for winter as well! As much as everyone loves winter comfort food, it is always nice to mix it up with something light and refreshing. Using a combination of frozen veggies and year-round cabbage, this is a refreshing and energizing dinner you can enjoy year round. Just in case you were wondering, soba noodles are Asian buckwheat noodles that just taste amazing! They are quick cooking, made from whole grains, and are much tastier than traditional whole wheat pastas. They can be found in the Asian section of most major supermarkets, local Asian markets, and online. Again, because seafood quickly spoils, this recipe is about four servings. The leftovers make a nice lunch the next day, but are not meant to be savored all week long.

For the stir-fry:

1	lb shelled and deveined uncooked shrimp	1	cup frozen corn kernels
6	oz soba noodles, about a 2-inch diameter	2	scallions
		1	tbsp extra virgin olive oil
1	small head savoy cabbage	1	tsp garlic salt
1	cup frozen peas	Sriracha hot chili sauce, if desired

For the marinade:

2	tbsp sesame oil	½	tsp white pepper
2	tbsp soy sauce	½	tsp black pepper
¼	cup organic sugar	1	tbsp cornstarch
1	tbsp ground ginger	2	tbsp filtered water
2	tsp garlic powder		

This is one of our family's favorite dinners. It comes together quickly, the ingredients are available year round, and it is full of healing nutrients. The only thing we do differently for the girls, is leave off the green onions and cut their shrimp into small pieces. They love slurping up the noodles and even eat some of the cabbage! Vegetarians can marinate extra firm tofu in place of the shrimp. When prepared using gluten-free soy sauce and 100% buckwheat soba noodles (some brands mix in wheat flour), this dish is gluten-free. Those sensitive to nuts can proceed as written.

Instructions:

Marinate the shrimp: Dissolve 1 tbsp cornstarch into 2 tbsp water. Add additional ingredients listed under "for the marinade". Toss with 1 pound peeled and deveined shrimp. Marinate for at least 15 minutes or up to 1 hour.

Prep your produce: Thinly slice 1 small head savoy cabbage (or ½ large) and 2 scallions. Measure out 1 cup each of frozen peas and corn.

> **Prince to pauper:** If you are trying to stretch your family's food dollar, buy shrimp that you need to peel and devein yourself. It is really quite simple. After peeling, take a small paring knife and make a slit down the front and back of each shrimp. Use your thumbnail to remove the vein. It takes a few extra minutes, but saves a few extra dollars!

Cook your soba noodles: Boil soba noodles in salted, boiling water for time indicated on package (about 4 minutes). Drain and immediately rinse with cool water to stop the cooking process. (This is extremely important for soba noodles. They will get soggy if you let them sit for even a minute.)

At the same time you begin heating the water for the noodles, start your stir-fry: Heat a large deep skillet over medium high heat for about 5 minutes. Add 1 tbsp olive oil and heat an additional 30 seconds, until oil shimmers. Place **peas** and **corn** in skillet. Stir-fry for about a minute. Next, add the **cabbage** and stir-fry a minute or two more. Finally, add the **shrimp and remaining marinade.** As soon as the shrimp are pink and opaque, about 2 – 3 minutes, reduce heat to medium.

Pulling it all together: Add cooked soba noodles and 1 tsp garlic salt to skillet. Toss until dish is heated throughout, about a minute. If desired, add additional sesame oil or soy sauce to taste. Transfer to a serving dish or divide among plates. Garnish with scallions. Pass Sriracha hot sauce at the table, if desired. Serve and enjoy!

The next time I make this, I'm going to try..._____

My actual cooking times for this dish were..._____

I'm going to share this recipe with..._____

Popeye Manicotti
from the kitchen of Marsha Boyer (my mommy)

START TO FINISH: 1 HOUR, 10 MINUTES ACTIVE.

This is a recipe from my childhood that we make again and again. It is super healthy, super easy, freezes exceptionally well, and tastes great! Because most manicotti shells are sold in packs of 12, always stuff at least 12 of these at a time. Before baking, freeze the extra stuffed shells for an "I need dinner" night. (Right before Ellie was born, we actually stocked our freezer with over three dozen!) Popeye manicotti is also a great dish for entertaining. Because everything can be done in advance, you will get to spend your time enjoying your guests, not scurrying around in the kitchen. When considering how many shells to bake, two stuffed shells is a generous adult size portion. For our family, we bake six at a time in an 8 x 8 glass baking dish. There is usually a little leftover for lunch. On nights that Darren gets stuck at the restaurant, I pull just three out, and bake them in a loaf pan.

1	pkg manicotti shells	1	cup cottage cheese
1	lb chopped frozen spinach	2	scallions
		1	tsp dried basil
1	cup shredded mozzarella	½	tsp sea salt
½	cup Parmigiano-Reggiano	½	tsp black pepper
Jarred pasta sauce, see below			

How do I know how much sauce to use?

3 shells in a loaf pan = 1¼ cups
6 shells in an 8 x 8 inch dish = 2¼ cups
12 shells in a 13 x 9 inch dish = 5 cups

This may seem like a lot of sauce, but do not skimp! The uncooked manicotti shells need it to get nice and tender. We usually just enjoy this as a one-dish meal (veggies, protein, and healthy carbs), but you may want to add a simple green salad and crusty bread if entertaining. These manicottis are naturally vegetarian and free of any nuts or nut products. Go gluten-free by using gluten-free shells. Oh yes, they are also incredibly kid-friendly. Both of my girls gobble these up!

Instructions:

If baking immediately after stuffing shells, preheat oven to 350 degrees.

Prep your produce: Thinly slice 2 scallions. Defrost chopped spinach. Use a kitchen towel to squeeze out all excess moisture.

> **Quick tip!!!** It is very important that you squeeze out all of the water from the spinach. Otherwise, your sauce will get watery. I usually squeeze my spinach with a second (dry) towel just to be sure.

Prepare your filling, and stuff your shells: Excluding the manicotti shells and pasta sauce, combine all remaining ingredients in a large mixing bowl. Using a spoon or clean hands, divide the filling among the 12 manicotti shells. If freezing shells for a future use, you are now ready to transfer the stuffed shells to the freezer. (uncooked.)

Bake your manicotti: Spread ½ cup (or 1 cup) of the pasta sauce onto the bottom of 8 x 8 (or 13 x 9) inch baking dish (to prevent noodles from sticking). Arrange 6 stuffed manicotti shells in dish. Top with remaining 2 cups (or 4 cups) pasta sauce. Sprinkle with additional mozzarella cheese to your preference. I use about ¼ cup. (If baking all 12 shells, use the measurements in parenthesis.) Cover dish with foil and bake at 350 degrees for 40 minutes. Remove foil and bake for an additional 10 minutes, until cheese is hot and bubbly. Remove from oven.

Getting it on the table: Allow manicotti to cool for about 5 minutes. Serve and enjoy!

> **Reminder:** To avoid potentially harmful additives and preservatives, buy organic pasta sauce. If that is not an option for you, check the ingredients to make sure that the manufacturers are not using high fructose corn syrup or corn sugar as the sweetener.

The next time I make this, I'm going to try..._____

My actual cooking times for this dish were..._____

I'm going to share this recipe with..._____

Moroccan Spiced (Chicken) Sausage
And Vegetable Couscous

START TO FINISH: 50 MINUTES, 15 MINUTES ACTIVE

Are you wondering where this idea came from? Chicken sausages were on sale, grilled sausage and vegetables rock, and we'd been talking about creating a Moroccan dish for quite awhile. When it came time to fire up the grill, the heat index was 110 degrees, and I felt guilty making Darren cook outside. Everyone loves roasted vegetables, so we decided to try roasting the sausages alongside the veggies. This dinner turned out awesome!!! (Seriously, the first attempt needed no alterations!) Aren't you excited that you can now enjoy the flavor of grilled sausage and veggies all year long? Chicken apple sausages really compliment the savory Moroccan spices, but whatever your favorite variety is should work just as well. Roasted and salted pepitas (pumpkin seeds) was the perfect addition of nuttiness and crunch (kind of like me)!

4	links chicken apple sausage (4 oz each)	3	tbsp extra virgin olive oil, divided
1	red bell pepper	1	lemon, zest and juice
1	small red onion	¼	cup pepitas
2	cups cremini mushrooms	¼	cup golden raisins
1⅓	cup whole wheat couscous	¼	cup cilantro
1⅓	cup chicken broth		

Seasonings:

1	tsp garlic powder	¼	tsp sweet paprika (aka Hungarian)
1	tsp ground cumin		
½	tsp ground coriander	⅛	tsp ground cayenne
½	tsp ground ginger	1	tsp sea salt
¼	tsp ground cinnamon	½	tsp black pepper

Once Annie understood that sausages are really just apple hot dogs, she chowed. To keep the mess to a minimum, I stir plain yogurt into the girls' couscous. Vegetarians, you can either use your favorite meat-free sausage, or double the veggies and omit the sausage all together. This dish is gluten-free by using quinoa in place of the couscous, and by verifying that there are no gluten ingredients in your brand of sausage. This dish is naturally free of nuts and any nut products. (Double check the ingredients on the sausages.) Serves four.

Instructions:

Preheat oven to 425 degrees for about 10 minutes.

While oven heats, prepare your seasonings and vegetables: In a small bowl or ramekin, combine all ingredients listed under "seasonings". Remove the stem, seeds, and ribs of 1 red bell pepper. Peel 1 small red onion. Cut bell pepper and onion into 1 inch pieces (approximately). Toss peppers and onions with all but 1 tsp of the combined seasonings. Toss again with 1 tbsp of extra virgin olive oil. Line a rimmed baking sheet with aluminum foil. Pour peppers and onions onto one half of the baking sheet. When oven is preheated, roast peppers and onions for 10 minutes.

While peppers roast, prepare your mushrooms and sausage: Wipe any visible dirt from mushrooms and quarter. Toss with remaining teaspoon of seasoning and an additional tablespoon extra virgin olive oil. Remove sausages from packaging and pierce each one with a fork 3 - 4 times. When 10 minutes have lapsed, remove peppers and onions from oven. Place whole chicken sausages and quartered mushrooms on the remaining fourths of the baking sheet. Return to oven and roast all ingredients for 20 minutes.

Prepare your couscous, finish your veggies and sausages: When the 20 minutes have lapsed, turn sausages, and stir vegetables. Return baking sheet to oven for the remaining 10 minutes of roasting. In a small saucepan, bring 1⅓ cup of chicken broth just to a boil. Remove from heat and stir in 1⅓ cup whole wheat couscous and cover pan with a tight fitting lid. Let couscous stand for 5 minutes, then fluff with a fork. After fluffing, stir in remaining 1 tbsp olive oil, pepitas, golden raisins, lemon zest and juice, and ¼ tsp each sea salt and fresh ground black pepper. Remove vegetables and sausages from oven and let stand just a couple minutes.

Getting it on the table: While the sausages rest, coarsely chop ¼ cup cilantro leaves. Toss couscous with peppers, onions, and mushrooms. Thinly slice sausages. Pour Moroccan spiced vegetable couscous onto a large serving platter. Top with sausage, and garnish with cilantro leaves. Serve and enjoy!

The next time I make this, I'm going to try..._____

My actual cooking times for this dish were..._____

I'm going to share this recipe with..._____

Salsa Verde Enchiladas

START TO FINISH: 15 MINUTES ACTIVE, 30 MINUTES BAKE TIME

The first time I made this for dinner, Darren's eyes lit up. As he piled his plate with a second portion, he exclaimed, "Obviously, this recipe will NOT be going in the cookbook. "I did it!!! I healthified green enchiladas in a way that fooled even my hubby! Do you want to know the secret? We eat with our eyes first. What did he see as he sat down to dinner? Brown, bubbly, ooey-gooey cheese. He was so excited about digging into this tasty dinner that he never noticed that the actual enchiladas were cheese (and cream) free. As far as the cabbage, nobody noticed, but me! If entertaining a crowd, you may double the recipe and assemble in a 13 x 9 inch baking dish. These enchiladas freeze beautifully, can be assembled up to a day ahead, and make an excellent lunch the next day. Serves four to six.

For the enchiladas:

3	cups cooked and shredded chicken (about 1 pound)	1½	cups Monterrey Jack
4	whole wheat tortillas (8-inch)	3	green onions
14	oz can your favorite green enchilada sauce	4	oz can green chilies
		¾	cup salsa verde
		½	cup sour cream
2	cups chopped Savoy cabbage	1	avocado

For the seasonings:

2	tsp ground cumin	¼	tsp cinnamon
½	tsp ground coriander	¼	tsp sea salt
½	tsp garlic powder	½	tsp black pepper

Much to my surprise, Annie and Ellie have been enjoying this meal since I first began making it (Ellie after nine months). When serving children, be sure to source brands of enchilada sauce and salsa verde that are labeled "mild". If you enjoy a little spice in life, green Tabasco is the perfect accompaniment. Vegetarians can double the avocado and omit the chicken. Those sensitive to gluten can substitute brown rice tortillas. (Food for Life makes a yummy option.) Otherwise, you may both proceed as written. This dish is naturally free of nuts and nut products.

Instructions:

Prepare your ingredients: Chop 2 cups Savoy (or Napa) cabbage. Thinly slice 3 green onions. Reserve 2 tbsp green onion for garnish. Place remaining green onion in a mixing bowl. Add green enchilada sauce, ¾ cup salsa verde, green chiles (undrained), sour cream, and all ingredients listed under "for the seasonings". Whisk until well combined.

Assemble your enchiladas: Spread ½ cup of the green sauce on the bottom of an 8 x 8 inch baking dish (to prevent tortillas from sticking). Just before assembling, thinly slice 1 avocado. Using clean hands, dip whole wheat tortillas into green sauce. Allow excess sauce to drip off each tortilla and then transfer to a dinner plate. Place about ¼ of the chicken, ¼ of the cabbage, ¼ of the avocado, and ¼ of the green sauce in each tortilla. Roll and place seam side down in your baking dish. Top entire dish with 1 cup Monterrey Jack cheese.

When it comes to storage: Once enchiladas are assembled, you may cover them and refrigerate up to one day, freeze them in a labeled and dated freezer bag for up to three months, or pop them in the oven for (almost) instant gratification.

Ingredient tip! When purchasing prepared enchilada sauce, try to avoid purchasing brands that contain ingredients you don't recognize as real food. Also, please note that this recipe calls for a 14 (or 15) ounce can of sauce. If your can is larger, measure out 1¾ cups and freeze the rest for a future use.

Baking your enchiladas: Preheat oven to 350 degrees. When baking your enchiladas immediately after assembling, bake uncovered for 30 minutes. Refrigerated enchiladas should be baked uncovered for about 40 minutes. Enchiladas prepared from frozen should be baked covered with foil for 30 minutes, and then uncovered for an additional 20 – 30 minutes, until piping hot throughout. After baking, transfer enchiladas to the broiler for 2 minutes to get cheese browned and bubbly. Serve and enjoy!

The next time I make this, I'm going to try..._____

My actual cooking times for this dish were..._____

I'm going to share this recipe with..._____

Beef and Vegetable Chinese Noodles

Technique shared by Fenche Shen

My friend Fenche always shows up to playdates with the most amazing stir-fried noodle dishes. Whenever we ask for the recipe, she laughs and says, "There is no recipe! You just throw it all together!" After trying and trying to pick her brain, I finally realized that I just needed to watch her do it. I cordially invited myself into her home to watch her cook. Thankfully, she obliged. Let me tell you, her version of measuring made my head spin! After scribbling notes fast and furiously, I headed home to create my own version of the amazing food she regularly feeds her family. (Yes, it took me several attempts.) By the way, we all laughed when we learned that her "Chinese noodles" were just overcooked spaghetti!

For the stir-fry:

¾	lb sirloin steak	8	oz spaghetti noodles
1	carrot	½	cup chicken broth
1	cup frozen peas	½	tsp garlic salt
1	cup frozen corn kernels	1	tbsp mushroom flavored
½	head Savoy (or Napa) cabbage		(or dark) soy sauce
3	green onions		Hot chili sauce, if desired

For the marinade:

3	tbsp sesame oil	1	tsp garlic powder
2	tbsp soy sauce	½	tsp black pepper
¼	cup organic sugar	¼	tsp crushed red pepper
1	inch piece ginger	¼	cup filtered water
1	tbsp organic peanut butter	1	tbsp cornstarch

This is a very kid-friendly dinner and great way to dress up veggies. I wrote the recipe for the marinade to be very mild (which is why I suggest hot chili sauce as an accompaniment). If your family is toddler free, feel free to increase the amount of crushed red pepper. Vegetarians can omit the steak, and substitute vegetable broth for chicken broth. Those with nut allergies can use a tablespoon of sunflower seed butter or tahini (ground sesame seeds) in place of the peanut butter. When made with gluten-free spaghetti noodles and gluten-free soy sauce, those sensitive to gluten can proceed as written. Serves four to six.

Instructions:

Prepare your marinade and get the steak marinating: Whisk 1 tbsp corn starch with ¼ cup water until dissolved. Whisk in all remaining ingredients listed under "for the marinade". Add steak to marinade, and stir to combine. Let steak marinate for 15 minutes or up to one day. (Store covered in the refrigerator if not using within the hour.)

Cook your noodles: Cook spaghetti in a large pot of salted, boiling water for two minutes longer than time indicated on package. Drain and immediately rinse with cool water to stop the cooking process. Allow to rest in colander until ready to add to skillet.

While the water comes to a boil, prepare and measure all other ingredients: Thinly slice ½ a head of cabbage and 3 green onions. Peel, trim, and shred (or dice) carrots. Measure out 1 cup each frozen peas and corn kernels. Measure out ½ cup of chicken broth.

When the spaghetti goes into the boiling water, start your stir-fry: Heat a large deep skillet or wok over medium high heat for about 5 minutes. When hot, add steak and remaining marinade to skillet. Sear steak for 1 - 2 minutes per side, until it can be turned without tearing. Next, add your carrots, peas, and corn to the skillet. Stir-fry for an additional 1 to 2 minutes. (It is important to add the ingredients slowly so the skillet stays hot, that is the trick to this quick cooking method.) Now, add the cabbage, and stir-fry until it has wilted down, about 1 minute more. Reduce heat to medium. Add cooked spaghetti, ½ cup chicken broth, and ½ tsp garlic salt to the beef and veggie mixture. Toss all ingredients until noodles are warm and coated with the sauce. Turn off heat. If desired, add 1 tbsp mushroom flavored dark soy sauce (or sesame oil to taste).

Getting it on the table: Transfer contents of skillet to a serving bowl. Garnish with green onions. Use tongs for easiest serving. Serve and enjoy!

The next time I make this, I'm going to try..._____

My actual cooking times for this dish were..._____

I'm going to share this recipe with..._____

Braised Chicken, Fennel, and Tomatoes
prepared in a parmesan infused broth over brown rice

START TO FINISH: 25 MINUTES, MOSTLY INACTIVE

This dinner is the perfect example of how a few high quality ingredients come together with simple preparations to create a flavorful, easy, and healthy dinner your whole family will adore. (You really do just throw everything into a skillet with a lid.) This is a great meal to make on nights you are entertaining, but not for dinner. It requires little cleaning, little prep, and is packed with nutrients. That means you don't have to spend much time getting the kitchen cleaned up before friends arrive to watch movies, drink wine, or play games. This dinner is packed with nutrients, light on fat and calories, and full of flavor. Evening gatherings always seem to involve some sort of treat. Eating this meal before hand will leave you with a little wiggle room to satisfy your sweet tooth!

1	lb boneless skinless chicken breast	½	cup dry white wine
1	large fennel bulb	1	tbsp extra virgin olive oil
1	pint cherry tomatoes	½	tsp + ½ tsp sea salt
½	cup Parmigiano-Reggiano	½	tsp + ½ tsp black pepper
		3	cups cooked brown rice

¼ cup reserved fennel fronds   ¼ cup pine nuts
Smoked paprika, small pinch for color

> If you are new to working with fennel, please do not be intimidated. Chop off the stems and then core it like cabbage. Once I overcame my "prep" insecurities, fennel quickly became one of my favorite veggies! As for the fronds, those are the little dill looking things growing from the stalks.

Both my girls love this simple dinner. You are basically steaming the chicken and infusing it with flavor. This keeps it super moist and kid-friendly. This dish is naturally gluten-free. Those sensitive to nuts can omit the pine nuts, but otherwise proceed as written. Vegetarians can omit the chicken and add 2 – 3 cups of prepared white beans to the vegetable mixture. The beans will absorb the flavors just as well as the chicken. Serves four.

Instructions:

Prep your produce: Core, trim, and thinly slice your fennel. Reserve about ¼ cup of the fronds for garnish. Halve one pint cherry or grape tomatoes.

Braise your chicken and vegetables: Place fennel and tomatoes into a large skillet with lid. Pour ½ cup each white wine and Parmigiano-Reggiano on top. Drizzle vegetables with 1 tbsp extra virgin olive oil, and season with ½ tsp each sea salt and fresh ground black pepper. Lay chicken breasts on top of vegetables. Season chicken breasts with an additional ½ tsp each sea salt and fresh ground black pepper. Cover with lid. Using high heat, bring mixture just to a boil. Reduce heat to medium-low, and simmer covered for 15 – 20 minutes, until chicken reaches an internal temperature of 165 degrees.

Pulling it all together: Transfer chicken from skillet to cutting board, and let rest for a couple minutes. Arrange hot rice on a serving platter. Pour contents of skillet over rice. Slice chicken, and lay on top of vegetables. Garnish with ¼ cup pine nuts and fennel fronds. Dust a bit of smoked paprika over the entire dish for eye appeal. Serve and enjoy!

Pinch more pennies...

As I've mentioned before, making and freezing your own brown rice is one of my favorite money saving tips. Those precooked pouches are way overpriced! Slicing larger chicken breasts is another great way to keep your friends and family from feeling deprived when it comes to their portion of meat. If your family does not regularly enjoy drinking white wine, take advantage of the individual bottles often sold in the refrigerated wine section (for less than $2.00). After all, there is no need to waste a whole bottle!

The next time I make this, I'm going to try..._____

My actual cooking times for this dish were..._____

I'm going to share this recipe with..._____

Cheesy Spinach and Mushroom Noodle Bake

START TO FINISH: 1 HOUR, PLUS BAKE TIME

This is another one of those amazing dinners that can be completely assembled up to a day in advance. It freezes beautifully, is a great cold day comfort food, and is fancy enough for entertaining. Fresh spinach, two types of mushrooms, and a rich creamy cheese sauce (that contains neither cream nor butter) come together to create a healthified version of the classic casseroles we all know and love. If you have friends or family members that believe no meal is complete without meat, this will surely prove them wrong!

For the noodle bake:

1	lb farfalle pasta	1	red onion
1	lb cremini mushrooms	¼	cup chicken broth
8	oz shitake mushrooms	⅓	cup dry sherry
9	cups fresh spinach	2	tbsp extra virgin olive oil
1	tbsp fresh thyme leaves, from about 1 package	2	tsp sea salt
8	cloves garlic, ½ head	2	tsp black pepper
4	cups whole milk	½	cup white whole wheat flour (or unbleached all-purpose)
1½	cups shredded asiago cheese		

For the cheesy, crunchy topping:

1	cup whole wheat panko breadcrumbs	2	tbsp extra virgin olive oil
1	cup shredded asiago cheese	1	tsp sea salt
¼	cup Parmigiano-Reggiano	1	tsp black pepper

This recipe serves eight to twelve. I usually fill two 8 x 8 inch baking dishes. For one of them, I use a disposable foil dish. I then pop it into a labeled and dated freezer bag and stash it in the freezer for a future dinner. One 8 x 8 generously feeds our family with plenty of leftovers. If you are a larger family or are entertaining guests, bake the entire recipe in a 13 x 9 inch dish. This also makes a great holiday potluck dish. It tastes fabulous alongside a gorgeous prime rib or beautiful bird.

Instructions:

Prepare your produce: Remove stems from shitake mushrooms (too tough) and slice in ¼ to ½ inch strips. Quarter cremini mushrooms. Coarsely chop spinach. Dice 1 red onion and mince 8 cloves of garlic. Coarsely chop the leaves and tender stems of enough fresh thyme to make 1 tbsp. If using block cheese, grate 2½ cups asiago.

> If this seems like a lot of vegetables for two simple dinners, that's because it is! The beauty of mushrooms and spinach is that they shrink considerably when cooked. This makes it easy to get your family to eat more veggies than they would if you served them raw. Did you realize there is almost a cup of spinach in every serving? Popeye would be proud!

Make your cheesy, crunchy topping: In a mixing bowl, combine 1 cup whole wheat panko breadcrumbs, 1 cup of the asiago cheese, ¼ cup Parmigiano-Reggiano, 2 tbsp extra virgin olive oil, and 1 tsp each sea salt and black pepper. Set aside.

Prepare your farfalle: In a large pot of salted boiling water, cook pasta one minute shy of package directions. Drain and rinse with cool water to stop the cooking process. Drain well, but do not return noodles to pot.

At the same time your pasta water is heating, start your sauté: Heat a large deep skillet over medium high heat for about five minutes. When skillet is hot, add 2 tbsp extra virgin olive oil and heat for an additional 30 seconds, until oil shimmers. Add onion and garlic to skillet and sauté for about 3 minutes. Add mushrooms, 2 tbsp chicken broth, and 2 tsp each sea salt and black pepper to onion and garlic. If mushrooms are starting to stick to skillet, add the additional 2 tbsp of chicken broth. (Sometimes I need it, sometimes I don't. It depends on the water content of the mushrooms.) Sauté for an additional 7 – 10 minutes, until mushrooms are nicely browned and have cooked down considerably. Pour ⅓ cup dry sherry and chopped thyme over mushrooms and stir for an additional 2 minutes, until the liquid has reduced by about half. Reduce heat to medium low and stir spinach into mushrooms until it is wilted and well combined. Turn off heat.

Prepare your cheese sauce: Heat your now empty pasta pot over medium high heat. Pour in 4 cups whole milk and ½ cup flour. Whisk constantly until mixture comes to a boil. Once boiling, continue whisking for an additional 2 – 3 minutes, until your sauce no longer smells like flour. Remove from heat. Whisk remaining 1½ cups asiago into sauce until melted.

Pulling it all together: Return pasta to its cooking pot and the cheese sauce. Add veggie mixture. Stir to combine and distribute ingredients throughout. Divide contents of pot equally between two 8 x 8 inch baking dishes (or one 13 x 9). Top each dish with half of the topping. Cover disposable 8 x 8 with foil and place in a labeled and dated freezer bag. Cover the other dish with plastic wrap and refrigerate until ready to bake.

Baking your noodle bake: Preheat oven to 375 degrees. If baking your pasta directly after assembling, bake uncovered for about 25 minutes. If baking your pasta from the refrigerator, bake uncovered for about 40 minutes. If baking your pasta from the freezer, bake covered with foil for the first 30 minutes. Remove foil and bake for an additional 20 – 30 minutes, until cheese sauce is hot and bubbly and the topping browned and crunchy. Let rest for 5 minutes before serving. Serve and enjoy!

Ingredient notes: Does it seem like this recipe contains too much salt? I've been there! Raw ingredients don't contain the sodium that prepared processed foods do. When I first started cooking real food, I always seemed to under season things. Once I understood why, it all made sense! For example, one serving of cream of mushroom soup contains almost 900 milligrams of sodium. The added salt in one serving of my noodle bake (1/12 of recipe) contains about half of that (or less than 20% of the daily RDA). This dish is naturally nut-free and easily goes vegetarian when vegetable broth is used in place of chicken broth. It goes gluten-free when you use brown rice fusilli in place of the farfalle, 1 cup of crushed 100% corn flakes (non-GMO) in place of the panko breadcrumbs, and ½ cup of rice flour to thicken the cream sauce. My kiddos both really enjoy this dinner (especially the pasta "bows") and the leftovers taste great!

The next time I make this, I'm going to try..._____

My actual cooking times for this dish were..._____

I'm going to share this recipe with..._____

Pozole Rojo

START TO FINISH: 11 HOURS, 15 MINUTES ACTIVE

The winter before blogging about Pozole Verde (the first recipe that got Healthnut Foodie some national attention), we developed this amazing recipe for Pozole Rojo. It was so hearty, easy, and satisfying that we immediately knew it would be going in the cookbook. In case you were wondering, pozole (po-SOE-lay) is a traditional pork and hominy Mexican stew that is synonymous with the word "fiesta". Often served at parties, this peasant stew is a great way to stretch your entertaining food bill. Authentic chefs take simple ingredients and let them simmer away on the stove for many hours, sometimes even days. We decided that using our slow cooker could give pozole the perfect modern day makeover. The results were phenomenal. If you are just feeding your small family, freeze half of the soup for a future dinner. This recipe makes enough for eight to ten generous bowls of pozole.

For the pozole rojo:

1	- 1¼ lb pork tenderloin	¼	cup ancho chili powder
3	cans of white hominy	2	tbsp Mexican oregano
1	large onion, any color	4	tsp sea salt
8	cloves garlic (½ head)	1	tsp black pepper
2	tbsp butter	8	cups filtered water

Garnishments:

¼	head green cabbage	1	bunch radishes
2	limes	½	wheel queso fresco
2	cups sour cream	1	bunch cilantro
Sriracha hot chili sauce, if desired			

The first time we made pozole, we were all surprised by how much Annie enjoyed it. The tender pork and hominy won her over. Ancho chili powder is a very flavorful spice, but much more mild than the traditional chili powder blend. This makes it a great kid-friendly addition to your spice cabinet. Hominy is so hearty that vegetarians could easily omit the pork (or non-pork eaters could easily substitute chicken thighs). Pozole rojo is naturally gluten-free and nut-free. Winner, winner, pozole dinner!

Instructions:

Prepare your pozole: Dice 1 large (or 2 small) onions. Mince 8 cloves of garlic. Rinse and drain 3 cans of white hominy. Place all ingredients listed under "for the pozole rojo" in a 5 – 6 quart slow cooker. Turn slow cooker on lowest setting (but not warm). Allow the flavors to mingle and the pork to braise while you go about your day.

> **Ingredient note:** Queso fresco is a crumbly white Mexican cheese that is quickly gaining in popularity. I have successfully found it at Super Target, Whole Foods, and my local supermarket. The other half of the wheel can be frozen until the next time you make this recipe, or you can use it to garnish tacos, omelettes, or quesadillas.

Prepare your garnishments: Either immediately after starting your pozole or just before serving, shred about ¼ head of green cabbage (I like savoy), chop 1 bunch of cilantro (leaves and tender stems only), slice 1 bunch of radishes, and cut 2 limes into wedges. Crumble ½ a wheel of queso fresco. Pour sour cream into a small serving bowl. Nestle ingredients together on a serving platter. If preparing ingredients ahead of time, wait to chop cilantro until just before serving or it will wilt. Cover serving platter with plastic wrap and refrigerate until ready to serve.

Getting it on the table: When pozole has finished cooking, transfer pork loin to a rimmed baking sheet (to keep the juices from spilling all over the counter). Use two forks (it is really that tender) to shred the pork. Return meat to slow cooker and stir to evenly distribute meat. Ladle soup into bowls and pass the garnishments at the table, instructing each guest to top their pozole with a lime (crucial to brighten the flavor) and whatever other accompaniments look good to them (I highly recommend them all). Serve and enjoy!

> If your family celebrates Christmas, the pretty red and green colors of this dish make it perfect for serving on Christmas Eve.

The next time I make this, I'm going to try..._____

My actual cooking times for this dish were..._____

I'm going to share this recipe with..._____

Santa Fe Chicken Salad

As much as we all turn to soups and stews to help get us through the winter, there is still a need for main dish salads. This Santa Fe chicken salad is the perfect winter salad, mostly because all of the ingredients are readily available year round. The dressing is a snap to make. The chicken and black beans are loaded with protein. The salsa and tomatoes offer a generous dose of lycopene, and the romaine lettuce gives the whole thing a nice crunch. Because leftover salad rarely gets eaten, this salad is just enough to generously serve two adults and a toddler. If your family is larger, double or triple the ingredients.

For the salad:

1	cup cooked shredded chicken	½	cup cherry tomatoes
1	cup prepared black beans	½	cup cilanto
1	cup frozen corn kernels, defrosted	6	cups romaine lettuce, (one 9-oz bag)
½	of an avocado	½	cup Monterrey Jack
			Pinch smoked paprika

For the dressing:

2	tbsp prepared salsa	¼	tsp chili powder
2	tbsp sour cream	¼	of a lime
2	tsp mayonnaise	½	tsp sea salt
½	tsp ground cumin	¼	tsp black pepper
¼	tsp dried basil		

Whisk together all ingredients listed under "for the dressing". Just before serving, start your slicing and dicing. Halve cherry tomatoes. Coarsely chop cilantro. Cube ½ an avocado. Toss romaine lettuce, cilantro, and tomatoes with salad dressing. Transfer to a serving platter. Top with chicken, avocado, black beans, cheese, and corn. Garnish with a pinch of smoked paprika.

This kid-friendly salad is naturally gluten-free and nut-free. When made without the chicken, it is also vegetarian.

The next time I make this, I'm going to try..._____

My actual cooking times for this dish were..._____

I'm going to share this recipe with..._____

Company's Coming Pot Roast Dinner

START TO FINISH: 8½ HOURS, 30 MINUTES ACTIVE

When honeymooning in Napa Valley, I remember being surprised when Darren ordered pot roast off a menu. I was even more surprised after tasting it. The flavors were so complex and the gravy so savory that I couldn't get enough. While I don't remember exactly which restaurant he ordered it in, I clearly remember how the caramelized crust mingled with the great flavors of wine and herbs. My recreation of this "Napa Valley pot roast" is not what you grew up eating on Sundays after church. This is a pot roast that will transport you to days when life was simpler, and the living rich. What makes it even better? You make it in the slow cooker! Yup, that's right. After browning the meat, you throw it in the slow cooker, and walk away for the next 8 – 10 hours. Yea!

For the pot roast:

3½	lb chuck roast, preferably grass-fed	½	cup beef broth
		¼	cup red wine, I used red zinfandel
6	carrots		
4	baking potatoes	¼	cup flat leaf parsley
1	large onion	2	tbsp extra virgin olive oil

For the seasonings:

¼	cup unbleached all purpose flour	2	tsp garlic powder
		2	tsp sea salt
1	tbsp dried thyme	1½	tsp black pepper

> **Quick conversions:** If you decide to cut this recipe in half, 2 tbsp is half of ¼ cup (for the flour), and 1½ tsp is half of 1 tbsp (for the thyme).

While this is a huge recipe, the leftovers are so versatile that we make a whole batch even if we are just feeding our little family. You can shred the leftover beef and freeze it for a future use (cover it with beef broth), toss it with barbeque sauce for sandwiches, make shredded beef tacos, or even a quick beef and vegetable stew. The possibilities are endless. This dinner is super kid-friendly and is naturally nut-free. When prepared using gluten-free rice flour, it easily goes gluten-free as well. (Vegetarians, I'm sorry to say, I have no clue how you could possibly do this without beef.) This recipe easily serves ten to twelve.

Instructions:

Prepare your produce: Cut 4 potatoes into rustic chunks (about 1½ to 2 inches each). Trim, peel, and cut carrots into 2 - 3 inch sticks. Peel and wedge one large (or two small) red onion. Place all of the vegetables in crock pot, and add ¼ cup red wine and ½ cup beef broth.

Crust and brown your beef: Heat a large flat skillet over medium high heat for about five minutes. While skillet heats, combine all ingredients listed under "for the seasonings". Dip chuck roast into flour mixture and cover thoroughly. Pour remaining flour mixture over vegetables (to thicken and flavor the gravy). When skillet is hot, add 2 tbsp extra virgin olive oil and heat an additional 30 seconds, until oil shimmers. Sear meat for 3 - 4 minutes per side in the hot oil. You are going for a nice golden crust, don't rush it!

> **Quick tip!!!** You may be tempted to save time and skip browning the beef. Please don't! This crucial steps helps the pot roast stand out from the rest. Browning the meat in a skillet adds a great caramelized color and flavor that the slow cooker alone cannot deliver.

Start your slow cooker: Place browned roast on top of vegetables. Cover your slow cooker and set it on the lowest setting (not warm). Let the ingredients mingle and the roast braise for 8 - 10 hours.

Getting it on the table: Just before serving, use two forks to break the roast into chunks. Transfer roast and vegetables to a serving platter. Either spoon gravy directly over dish or pour into a gravy boat for serving. Garnish with fresh parsley. Serve and enjoy!

> **Waste not, want not:** Looking for a great recipe to use up some of the leftover parsley and beef? Check out our Fried Egg and Roast Beef Hash, listed under "Dinners for Spring".

The next time I make this, I'm going to try..._____

My actual cooking times for this dish were..._____

I'm going to share this recipe with..._____

Maple-Mustard Panko Chicken
on a bed of lemon-spinach linguini

START TO FINISH: 25 MINUTES, MOSTLY ACTIVE

This is Darren's favorite meal in this cookbook! Whenever I tell him we are having this for dinner, his face lights up. I love it! Basically, this is a healthified version of "fried" chicken topped with a sweet and savory maple-mustard sauce and then served on a bed of lemon-spinach linguini. Comfort food at its finest! Wilting spinach into the linguini is a great way to get your whole family to eat more greens, and the fresh lemon zest and juice will give your immune system a healthy boost. If your family is larger, double the ingredients for the chicken and sear the chicken in batches, being careful not to crowd the skillet. Serves four.

For the panko chicken:

1	lb boneless, skinless chicken breasts	½	tsp black pepper
1	egg	½	cup whole wheat panko breadcrumbs
2	tbsp Creole mustard	2	tbsp extra virgin olive oil
½	tsp sea salt		

For the maple-mustard sauce:

¾	cup chicken broth	3	tbsp real maple syrup
3	tbsp Creole mustard		

For the lemon-spinach linguini:

8	oz linguini (½ pkg)	2	tbsp walnut oil
5	oz fresh spinach (4 cups)	¼	tsp organic sugar
¼	cup Parmigiano-Reggiano	½	tsp sea salt
1	lemon, zest and juice	½	tsp black pepper

If you are trying to convince someone that real food rocks, make this dinner for him. Then reveal that it only costs about $10.00 (assuming you will use the remaining ingredients for future dinners). If that isn't convincing enough, I don't know what is! Vegetarians, you can easily substitute extra firm tofu steaks for the chicken, and use vegetable broth in place of the chicken broth. Those sensitive to nuts can use extra virgin olive oil in place of the walnut oil. Those sensitive to gluten can skip the breading process, seasoning the chicken with ¼ tsp each salt and pepper, and then searing the naked chicken in the hot oil.

Instructions:

Make your maple-mustard sauce: In a small bowl, whisk together all ingredients listed under "for the maple-mustard sauce.

Prepare your chicken: Place chicken breasts between two pieces of wax paper. Use a rolling pin to roll/pound out chicken until it is about ½ inch thick. Cut chicken into four to six similarly sized pieces. In a small bowl, whisk together 1 egg and 2 tbsp Creole mustard. In a second bowl, mix together ½ cup whole wheat panko breadcrumbs with ½ tsp each sea salt and black pepper.

Start your lemon-spinach linguini: Cook linguini in a large pot of salted boiling water according to the time indicated on package. While water heats, coarsely chop spinach. When linguini has finished cooking, drain and immediately rinse with cool water to stop the cooking process. Drain again.

Simultaneously, sear your chicken: Heat a large flat skillet over medium high heat for about 5 minutes. While skillet heats, dip each piece of chicken in the egg mixture and then coat with breadcrumbs. When skillet is hot, add 2 tbsp extra virgin olive oil and heat an additional 30 seconds, until oil shimmers. Place breaded chicken cutlets in hot oil and brown for about 4 minutes per side, until breadcrumbs are golden brown and chicken has reached an internal temperature of 165 degrees. Transfer chicken to a dinner plate to rest. Pour the maple mustard sauce into the now empty skillet, stirring up any remaining breadcrumbs and chicken bits from bottom of skillet. Boil sauce for 5 minutes to allow the sauce to thicken and reduce. Turn off heat.

Pulling it all together: While sauce is thickening, turn the burner under the now empty pasta pot to medium low. Return cooked linguini to pot and toss with all remaining ingredients listed under "for the lemon-spinach linguini". When spinach is wilted and pasta is reheated (1 – 2 minutes), turn off heat. Place a bed of lemon-spinach linguini on each plate and top with 1 – 2 pieces of chicken. Spoon a tablespoon or two of the sauce over each serving of chicken. Divide remaining sauce among small ramekins for dipping. Serve and enjoy!

The next time I make this, I'm want to try..._____

My actual cooking times for this dish were..._____

I'm going to share this recipe with..._____

White Chicken Chili

START TO FINISH: 1 HOUR 20 MINUTES, 20 MINUTES ACTIVE

A few years ago, my mom got me hooked on white chicken chili. She actually mailed me a little spice packet with a note saying, "You have got to make this." I loved it, Darren loved it, and it was super simple to prepare. I knew that the MSG, hydrolyzed this, and autolyzed that wasn't good for our health, but I really didn't care. It was that tasty. Then Annie got old enough to start eating table food. It turned out that she really liked white chicken chili! Shocked, we realized we had to figure out how to recreate this super tasty chili from scratch. (Sayonara tasty little packet.) Y'all, this recipe knocked it out of the park! Our white chicken chili is sure to become a part of your family's regular dinner rotation. Super comforting, super easy, and super economical, it generously serves four to six. Leftovers are fantastic.

For the chili:

3	cups cooked shredded chicken, about 1 lb	4	cloves garlic
3	cups prepared white beans, or two 15-oz cans	2	tbsp extra virgin olive oil
1½	cups frozen corn kernels	1	qt chicken broth
4	oz can diced green chilies	¼ - ½	cup sour cream
1	large yellow onion	3	green onions
		¼	cup flat-leaf parsley

For the seasonings:

1	tbsp ground cumin	1	tsp sea salt
1	tsp ground coriander	½	tsp black pepper
1	tsp dried oregano	⅛	tsp cayenne

This is a very flavorful soup, but has very little heat. That makes it super kid-friendly. Our entire family looks forward to this simple dinner. Vegetarians, omit the chicken and use vegetable broth in place of chicken broth. This dish is naturally nut-free and gluten-free. If you choose to double the recipe to freeze for a future dinner, freeze the second batch of soup before you stir in the sour cream (to prevent the cream from curdling when reheated). If you forget and add the sour cream, reheat the soup at just over medium low, no higher.

Instructions:

Prepare your ingredients: Dice 1 large or 2 small yellow onions. Mince 4 cloves garlic. Thinly slice 3 green onions. Coarsely chop ¼ cup flat leaf parsley. If necessary, drain and rinse white beans.

In a small bowl or ramekin, combine all ingredients listed under "for the seasonings".

Prepare your white chicken chili: Heat a 4 – quart or larger stockpot over medium heat for about 5 minutes. While pot heats, use a hand held blender or mini food processor to puree 1½ cups beans with 1 cup of the chicken broth (this will help thicken the soup). When pot is hot, add 2 tbsp extra virgin olive oil and heat an additional 30 seconds, until oil shimmers. Add diced onion and garlic and sauté for about 6 minutes. Add combined seasonings and stir continuously for 2 minutes, being mindful not to let the spices burn. Add remaining chicken broth, shredded chicken, whole beans, pureed beans, frozen corn, and green chilies to pot. Increase heat to bring just to a boil. Once boiling, reduce heat to medium low and simmer for about an hour. Remove from heat. Stir in green onions, parsley, and ¼ - ½ cup sour cream, until soup achieves the consistency you desire.

Getting it on the table: Ladle soup into bowls. Serve with your favorite whole grain crackers, fruit, or cut up veggies and dip. Enjoy!

The next time I make this, I'm going to try..._____

My actual cooking times for this dish were..._____

I'm going to share this recipe with..._____

To each and everyone of you that have chosen to join me on this real food adventure,

Thank You

and happy eating!!!

The Ingredients

It is imperative to me that you understand why I feed my family the way I do. Therefore, before I even share the recipes, I am going to explain to you why I've picked every ingredient used in this cookbook. Anytime you wonder why I use a certain ingredient (whether you think it is healthy or not), you can reference it here. I want my books and my life to be as open and honest as possible. Do I really think that bacon is a health food? Yes and no. While I wouldn't call it a superfood, a few slices of nitrate-free bacon adds a great flavor to an otherwise simple and healthy dish, while still keeping the overall fat and calorie count in check. When used in moderation, I do not believe it will cause any adverse health effects. Why do I think extra virgin olive oil is so much better than vegetable oil and canola oil? Extra virgin olive oil is full of antioxidants and healthy monounsaturated fat, nutrients most Americans are deficient in. Vegetable oil and canola oil is mostly genetically modified corn, soy, and canola that is full of omega-6 fatty acids. While okay in moderation, the average American has an omega-6/omega-3 ratio of 20:1. Ideally, it should be closer to 3:1.

In organizing the ingredients, I filed the information under the title that I believed would make the most sense to the masses. For example, "nitrate-free bacon" has been filed under "B" as opposed to "N". If your brain works differently than mine and you don't find an ingredient listed, try searching again using the secondary word.

I am not going to preach about the benefits of using organic, grass fed, omega-3 rich foods in every recipe. I understand that some people just want to cook. However, the information is here if you want it. Herbs and spices have some amazing, healing properties. Organic grass-fed beef is healthier for you than most fish, and the taste of free range, organic chicken makes you never want to eat conventional chicken again. These recipes are the meals that I have fed my family, and that I will continue to feed my family for many years to come. I assure you, my recipes are 100% free of trans fat, hydrogenated oils, genetically modified vegetable oils, genetically modified canola oils, high fructose corn syrup, artificial sweeteners, and artificial colors. If you struggle with weight issues, you may even lose a few pounds as you bring your body back into balance. I truly believe that following a diet similar to mine will help your family live longer, healthier, and more energetic lives.

Please, don't be a stranger! I want to help you improve your health and the world we live in. http://www.healthnutfoodie.com.

A

Acorn squash: This is a cute little squash that is widely available nationwide during the fall and winter months. The halves are great for stuffing, and are perfect for portion control. Nutritionally, acorn squash offers tons of vitamin A in the form of beta carotene. (That's actually where it gets its orange color.) It also contains generous amounts of vitamin C, potassium, manganese, and folate. Vitamin C improves the immune system, potassium helps regulate blood pressure, and folate can help prevent birth defects.

Almonds: Almonds are an amazingly healthy seed. (That's right; they are technically a seed, not a nut. Who knew?) Scientists have concluded that the high amounts of monounsaturated fatty acids found in almonds can help lower cholesterol. Almonds are also packed with manganese, vitamin E, and magnesium. Because almonds help stabilize blood sugar, eating them alongside sweets will help prevent the sugar high and crash effect, which occurs after eating sugar alone.

Ancho chili powder: Ancho chili powder is completely different from regular chili powder. It is a mild chili powder made from roasting poblano chilies. It adds a smokiness and depth of flavor to many Mexican dishes. If ancho chili powder is unavailable in your market, order it online. If you don't have access to the Internet, and still want to use a recipe calling for ancho chili powder, substitute equal parts smoked paprika and regular chili powder. (It works, but will change the flavor profile of the dish). Medicinally, ancho chilies have been used to relieve congestion, rev up the metabolism, and reduce cholesterol. They contain capsaicin, and vitamins A and C.

Arrowroot starch: Arrowroot starch (like corn starch) is a natural way to thicken sauces without adding fat or calories. Of all the starch thickeners, arrowroot starch is the lightest, and has the least amount of flavor. This makes it ideal for delicate sauces (like shrimp and soba) or seasonal fruit desserts. I like arrowroot starch because it is not made from genetically modified ingredients like corn starch often is. It is quickly gaining popularity and can be found at many supermarkets, health food stores, and online.

Marinated artichoke hearts: Marinated artichoke hearts are a great way to add a burst of flavor to an otherwise simple dish. Artichokes promote a healthy liver, help detoxify the body, and stabilize blood sugar. When purchasing artichokes, look for brands packed in olive oil. This will protect you from being exposed to potentially harmful genetically modified canola or vegetable oils. You can also source brands labeled "non-GMO" or "GMO-free".

Arugula: Arugula is a peppery green that is part of the cruciferous family. It is high in vitamins A, C, K and folic acid. It also contains high levels of potassium, calcium, and phytochemicals (which are known to help prevent cancer). Its amazing flavor compliments a wide range of foods including fennel, citrus, mushrooms, goat cheese, and beef. It is hands down one of my favorite salad greens!

Asparagus: Who doesn't giggle after eating asparagus? Whether eaten with a fork or as a finger food, this is one amazing vegetable. It is high in bone-building vitamin K, folate (which helps prevent birth defects), and is a natural diuretic. It can also help prevent the water weight gain associated with PMS, and can help reduce the swelling that accompanies rheumatoid arthritis.

Avocado: Besides being the perfect first food for babies, avocados add an amazing creaminess to just about any dish. When eaten with other produce, the healthy fat in avocadoes will help your body better absorb the fat-soluble nutrients contained in many fruits and vegetables. They are also high in glutathione. Glutathione can help slow aging and prevent cancer cells from multiplying.

B

Nitrate-free bacon: A few slices of bacon add an amazing depth of flavor to a meal. Always, always, always source nitrate-free bacon! Nitrates and nitrites (often listed as sodium nitrates on food labels) are a chemical preservative found in most processed meats (including deli meat, hot dogs, ham, bacon, smoked fish, and corned beef). When ingested, they mix with certain acids in your stomach to create nitrosamines. Many studies have shown that nitrosamines can cause stomach cancer, trigger migraines, and cause decreased lung function. The evidence against nitrates is so conclusive that other countries have banned them from being used all together. Does bacon makes you fat? Consider this, a tablespoon of bacon drippings has almost the exact same amount of calories, and grams of fat, as a tablespoon of extra virgin olive oil. Granted, half of the fat in bacon is saturated fat, but because I use it sparingly, I am completely okay with it!

Dried basil: Dried herbs are a shelf-stable, more affordable alternative to fresh. Luckily, most of the nutrients stay intact during the drying process. The only thing lost during the drying process is some of the volatile oils. Some brands add chemical preservatives to their dried herbs. Because of this, please source organic, or buy from a trusted source to avoid this danger. To substitute dried herbs for fresh, replace 1 tsp of dried herbs for 1 tbsp of fresh herbs. Also, be sure to add the dried herbs earlier on in the dish. It takes a bit longer for the dried herbs to release their flavor than fresh.

Fresh basil: Basil is another great way to add flavor and health to a variety of dishes. Just one tablespoon provides almost 100% of your daily vitamin K needs, as well as good amounts of iron, magnesium, and vitamin C. Basil has natural anti-bacterial properties, promotes good cardiovascular health, and helps reduce inflammation in the body. Basil is also very easy to grow at home, smells great, and looks pretty too!

Bay leaves: What exactly are bay leaves and why do you always have to take them out before serving? That's what I had been wondering for years! It turns out that the bay leaf is the leaf of the bay laurel tree. They offer a nice, slightly floral essence to soups, stews, and sauces, but have a pungent and bitter taste when bitten into. While simmering, the bay leaf seeps vitamin C, iron, and potassium into the rest of the dish. They can also be used to relieve digestive disorders, fight dandruff, and help bee stings. Who knew?

Beans, in general: Eating beans is one of the best things you can do for your health, your waistline, and your wallet. Beans stabilize blood sugar, are packed with antioxidants, have tons of fiber, cost just pennies a serving (especially when made from scratch), and are ready to adapt to any recipe. With all of the talk about the dangers of canned food, you may be turning away from canned beans. While it is healthier to make your own dry beans, I believe that the benefits and convenience of canned beans outweigh the risks. As I've mentioned, I make a whole bag of dried beans at a time and freeze them in 1½ cup increments in a bit of the cooking liquid. (This is the perfect substitution for a can of beans.) Below you will find the additional health benefits of the individual variety of beans.

Black beans: Black beans are special! They detoxify sulfites, lower cholesterol, and prevent spikes in blood sugar. When paired with brown rice, they create a complete protein. Black beans hold their shape when cooked, and work great in quesadillas, mashed, or as a way to replace half of the amount of beef in many Hispanic dishes. Regular consumption of black beans has also been known to lower your risk for heart disease.

Pinto beans: Pinto beans are a great source of folate, magnesium, and tryptophan. They are medium sized, beige beans that taste great in broth-y Spanish dishes, baked beans, or mashed as a dip. I like to mix mashed pinto beans with salsa, sour cream, and cheddar cheese for a simple appetizer (layer and then bake at 350 degrees for 20 minutes). Like other beans, pinto beans stabilize blood sugar, lower cholesterol, and promote a healthy weight.

Red beans: Like most red, deeply colored fruits and vegetables, red beans are full of antioxidants. They provide energy boosting iron, memory boosting niacin, and cardiovascular promoting magnesium. They offer about 15 grams of protein per cup (more than two eggs!), can help lower cholesterol, and aid in weight loss. Red beans taste great in curries, salads, and tossed with simple herbs, olive oil, and fresh lemon.

White beans: Also referred to as navy beans or cannelini beans, white beans are smaller beans that taste great in white chili and are often used as baking beans. They help stabilize blood sugar, add a great, starchy texture to a dish, and are full of fiber and protein. White beans can easily replace pasta in soups and stews, increasing protein while fighting heart disease.

Bean sprouts: Bean sprouts are an inexpensive way to bulk up pad Thai, make a dish a nutritional rock star, and provide a refreshing crunch. When purchasing, choose firm sprouts and avoid the ones that are turning brown. The Chinese have used sprouts medicinally for years. Sprouting the bean produces chlorophyll, which can help cure anemia. Sprouts are a living food, and one of the only foods that continue to develop nutrients after harvesting.

Grass-fed ground beef: Grass-fed beef is becoming more readily available, and is relatively inexpensive compared to many other animal proteins. For optimal health, we need to have an omega-6 to omega-3 ratio of less than 4:1. Grass-fed beef has an omega-6 to omega-3 ratio of 3:1, while grain-fed beef has a ratio of around 20:1 (similar to that of the typical American). Bringing down your ratio by eating less omega-6, and more omega-3, can help in the prevention and treatment of autoimmune disease, many types of cancer, obesity, and heart disease. (Do you feel like you are back in school? I had to reread that part several times too!) Switching to grass-fed beef is a simple way to help do so. Grass-fed beef is also higher in CLA (conjugated linoleic acid), which aids in weight loss (lose weight eating beef?!?), and helps prevent cancer and immune disorders. Grass-fed beef is almost always hormone and antibiotic free, primarily because the cattle are less prone to illness, and the farmers have a higher level of dedication to sustainable living. This is a direct result of being able to exercise, enjoy healthy greens, and breathe fresh, clean air. As far as fat content, grass-fed beef is also naturally leaner, usually weighing in at 7% to 10% fat content. It tastes amazing, is super tender, and is better for the planet. Source grass-fed beef from local farmers to take your efforts one step further, and to get the best quality for your dollar!

Organic beef broth: I always buy organic beef broth! To make beef broth, you basically let the carcass of the cow simmer away in water, allowing all remaining flavors to infuse the liquid. If the point of broth is to extract every last bit of flavor from the cow, where do you suppose the lingering growth hormones and antibiotics are going? Exactly. Additionally, many conventional brands add dangerous preservatives, additives, and flavorings that I would just prefer to avoid.

Roast beef: Roast beef is just that; beef roasted in an oven. Rump, round, or chuck all work for roast beef. Cook the roast low and slow to get the meat nice and tender. Because these cuts are inexpensive, I go grass-fed and make a few pounds at once. I then shred and freeze it for hash, sandwiches, quesadillas, or just plain old munching. If you choose to buy your roast beef at the deli counter, please make sure it is nitrate-free. My favorite pre-packaged is Applegate Farms organic grass-fed roast beef. It is more expensive, but tastes wonderful! Beef is also high in vitamins B12 (which helps fight depression), zinc (which can help boost fertility), and iron (which helps prevent anemia). Tender roast beef is a great dish for babies and toddlers, easy to chew, and high in crucial nutrients.

Organic bell pepper: Bell peppers are constantly on Environmental Working Group's dirty dozen list, so I try to source them organically whenever possible (or grow your own!). That being said, bell peppers are packed full of nutrients, whatever variety you choose. Bell peppers are sweet and crunchy, making them the perfect vegetable to dip in hummus. They contain antioxidants that can lessen the symptoms of asthma, help repair cell damage from the exposure to everyday toxins, and help promote cardiovascular health. One bell pepper provides almost 300% of the RDA of vitamin C and 100% of vitamin A.

Bibb lettuce: Also called butter lettuce, limestone lettuce, or Boston lettuce. This is a delicate, buttery variety of lettuce that makes a great bed for other salads. Bibb lettuce contains vitamin A and folic acid, a crucial nutrient for brain development. I always love to serve chicken salads on a bed of lettuce to make the portions appear larger and more attractive.

Ian's whole wheat panko breadcrumbs: Panko breadcrumbs add a great crunch to routine chicken and fish dinners. I use them to stretch the meat in meatballs, as well as a thickener for stuffing. I picked this brand and variety because in a blind taste test (that I personally conducted), no one could tell they were whole wheat. Whole wheat panko is also a great way to add more whole grains to your diet. For more information and where to buy: http://www.iansnaturalfoods.com/breadcrumbs.html. (No, they are not paying me...yet!)

Broccoli: Broccoli, as well as other members of the cruciferous family, is excellent at fighting cancer cells. It is believed that the sulforaphane found in broccoli can help reduce the size of malignant tumors. Broccoli is also thought to slow the aging process, and contains as much calcium as a glass of milk.

Broccolini: I find that this vegetable makes dishes a little more special as it is not something we consume everyday. The cost and nutrient profile is similar to that of broccoli. The stalks of broccolini (or baby broccoli) are thinner than broccoli, allowing it to cook quicker. In general, I also find that it is more user friendly. Broccolini is a good source of vitamin C, potassium, folate, and fiber. If broccolini is not available, feel free to substitute traditional broccoli florets.

Organic brown sugar: Organic brown sugar is tasty and available at Whole Foods, Trader Joe's, and in the health section of many national grocers. If you cannot find it, you can add 2 tbsp molasses to 1 cup regular organic sugar. Do not confuse organic brown sugar with turbinado sugar, or sugar in the raw. While both of these sugars are brown in color, they lack the depth of flavor true brown sugar provides. For more nutritional information, see "organic sugar".

Brussel sprouts: I love brussel sprouts! Seriously. When properly prepared they have a nice, nutty crunch and are packed with nutrients. The key to a tasty sprout is not to overcook it. If you haven't had a brussel sprout since childhood, please give them a second try. Basically mini cabbages, brussel sprouts can help detoxify the body, boost your immunity, and regulate your bowel system.

Butter: I used to be scared of butter. I thought that if I consumed it, I would get fat. (I'm serious.) Darren helped me realize that when used in modest portions, butter adds a flavor to many dishes that olive oil just can't match. Anytime you see butter in this cookbook, please know that I am using the smallest amount possible without compromising the complexity of the dish. Butter is basically just churned whole milk anyways. When possible, source butter made from cows not treated with growth hormones or upgrade to organic.

Butternut squash: Thanks to their thick skin, it is not necessary to pay the extra money for organic winter squash. That makes butternut squash a great inexpensive option for feeding your family. Their bright orange color tells us that these little gems are packed full of vitamin A in the form of beta carotene. An adequate supply of beta carotene boosts the immune system, supports a healthy reproductive system, and can help strengthen our cells from the damage caused by daily exposure to toxins. Butternut squash is also a good source of vitamin C, potassium, and fiber.

C

Green cabbage: I love cabbage! It is inexpensive, low in calories, and available year round. It also provides tons of bone building vitamin K, which many Americans are deficient in. The phytonutrients in cabbage naturally detoxify the body, and are great at fighting cancer cells.

Red cabbage: Thanks to its deep purple hue, red cabbage is higher in antioxidants and vitamin C than green. In my opinion, it is also a bit sweeter. As with all types of cabbage, I love the way it cooks down. This allows you to pack multiple servings of vegetables into one simple dinner. (When trying to decide which color of cabbage to pick, think about what other colors already exist in the dish you will be using it in.)

Savoy/Napa cabbage: Unlike its crunchy red and green cousins, Savoy (also Napa or Chinese) tastes more like a cross between cabbage and lettuce. It is virtually calorie free, and is a great way to bulk up stir-fries and fried rice dishes. It is high in immunity boosting vitamin C, and a great source of dietary fiber.

Capers: Capers are an unripened and pickled Mediterranean flower bud. They impart a salty, sweet, and savory flavor to many French and Italian dishes. Capers add a "special-ness" to a meal, are packed with antioxidants, and are a great immunity booster. Store in the refrigerator once opened.

Ground cardamom: Cardamom is an aromatic, floral, citrus-y herb that adds a certain "je ne sais quoi?" to a dish. It is native to India and the Middle East. Holistically, cardamom is used to naturally detoxify the body, regulate the digestive tract, and help with respiratory problems.

Organic carrots: Carrots are a staple in Western and European diets. They are inexpensive and appeal to kids and grown ups alike. They are loaded with beta-carotene, vitamins C and K, and folic acid. Organic carrots cost just pennies more than conventional. Please source organic whenever possible. Conventional carrots contain higher levels of nitrates due to the use of certain fertilizers.

Roasted cashews: Nuts are a great way to boost the nutrients, healthy fats, and taste of many dishes. People think that nuts are expensive, but a little goes a long way. When compared to most meats, they are still cheaper per pound. Cashews have high levels of magnesium (which can help fight fatigue), and are believed to help raise good cholesterol levels.

Ground cayenne pepper: Cayenne pepper, or capsaicin, is one of those spices that regularly get praised for its healing properties. It is a natural anti-inflammatory, revs the metabolism, and helps boost the immune system. It is a great way to improve your health, and (when used in proper proportions) doesn't necessarily make foods overly spicy. The wide variety of recipes I use this amazing spice in may surprise you.

Organic celery: Celery has long been respected for its medicinal properties. Studies have shown that including celery in your diet can lead to lower cholesterol and blood pressure levels. Celery is high in vitamins C and K, as well as a compound called phthalides (which help reduce stress). I source organic celery whenever available, as it is regularly on Environmental Working Group's dirty dozen list. High levels of chemical and pesticide exposure have been shown to raise the risk of breast cancer and weaken the immune system.

Celery salt: Celery salt is just that. Ground celery seeds mixed with salt. I tried to come up with a way to describe the aromatic taste of celery salt. I was at a loss for words. I then tried to find a good description on the internet, and still nothing. Medicinally, studies have shown that celery seed is a natural diuretic, can help cure and prevent urinary tract infections, and can fight off symptoms from the common cold and flu. It also tastes great and is virtually calorie free. So, then there's that.

Asiago cheese: Asiago cheese is an Italian cheese made from grass-fed cow's milk. It has a sharp, but creamy flavor that can enhance a variety of dishes. I love to use it on pizza, stir it into a risotto, or just eat it with crackers. Asiago is a great source of calcium, and when sourced from Italy, you can be sure that your cheese is pasture raised, not pumped full of hormones.

Cheddar cheese: Studies have shown that regularly consuming cheddar cheese can help you maintain a healthy smile. The enzymes in cheddar help to stimulate the flow of saliva, reducing the amount of bacteria in the mouth. When purchasing cheddar cheese, please source brands that are either organic or made from cows not treated with growth hormones. Growth hormones do just what they suggest: cause the cows to grow faster, fatter, and to produce more milk. Although the FDA disagrees, many studies have shown that consuming cows and cow products treated with hormones can lead to early puberty, childhood obesity, and other unwanted side effects.

Cottage cheese: Cottage cheese is a low fat, high protein cheese that is a great addition to any diet. Cottage cheese is a combination of fast burning whey and slow burning casein. This makes it a perfect snack when you need instant energy that can sustain you for hours. It is also inexpensive and full of riboflavin, vitamin B12, phosphorus, and selenium. Because the organic varieties of cottage cheese are two to three times more costly than the conventional, I choose to purchase brands that are made from cows free from rBGH and other artificial growth hormones. For a simple lunch, enjoy cottage cheese atop a bed of sliced heirloom tomatoes, sea salt, and freshly ground black pepper. I ate about of a pint of cottage cheese daily when pregnant with both of my girls. It was my ultimate cure for nausea and aversions.

Cream cheese: If you have kids, you've probably already realized that cream cheese is way more than just a topping for bagels. One of the best tricks I have for taking a dish from "too flavorful" to "kid friendly" is to add a couple ounces of cream cheese. One of Annie's favorite sandwiches is roast beef, cream cheese, pickles, and tomatoes. Here's the skinny on cream cheese: you can enjoy two huge, satisfying tablespoons for just 90 calories. That's 100 calories less than the equal amount of organic peanut butter. Cream cheese offers calcium, protein, and potassium. It is also a great low(er) fat way to impart a creamy, tasty flavor to food.

Gorgonzola cheese: Gorgonzola is a crumbly blue cheese that is made in the Piedmont or Lombardy regions of Italy. It is a great way to add flavor to vegetables, meats, or grains. Because it is such a pungent cheese, a little goes a long way. This makes it a wonderful cheese choice for those watching their wallets and their waistlines. If gorgonzola cheese is too strong for your taste, you may try substituting Cambozola, which is a very mild type of blue cheese. If that is still too strong, you might try feta or pecorino.

Goat cheese: I love goat cheese! It was actually one of the first foods I fed both of my babies. Goat cheese has a rich creamy texture, mild, but remarkable flavor, and is less likely to cause allergies than cow cheeses. It is high in calcium, potassium, and tryptophan. Tryptophan is thought to induce sleep and to relax the body. Goat cheese is a great topping for salad or pizza, can be stirred into a hearty bowl of soup, and makes excellent quesadillas.

Gruyere/Swiss cheese: Gruyere is a mild variety of Swiss cheese that is made in the town of Gruyeres in Switzerland. It is made from cow's milk, and when eaten young, has a smooth, nutty flavor. Gruyere cheese is a great way to jazz up a variety of dishes. It is high in bone building calcium, lower in sodium than most cheeses, and a good source of vegetarian protein. Unless you live near a Trader Joe's, Gruyere can be a bit costly. Feel free to substitute Emmentaler or baby Swiss if that is the variety on sale.

Monterey Jack cheese: Monterey Jack cheese was first made in the late 1700s by monks living on California's central coast. Monterey Jack has a mild flavor that appeals to kids of all ages. Like other varieties of cheese, it is a great source of minerals that can help support a healthy metabolism, and fight the progression of osteoporosis. Monterey Jack also contains CLA's, which can help prevent the cells that can cause cancer. Because Monterey Jack is made in the United States, it is important to look for brands that are hormone and antibiotic free. In a pinch, substitute mozzarella or Colby Jack. For a splurge, try upgrading to a smoked Jack. It is so tasty!

Mozzarella cheese: Mozzarella cheese is a staple in our home. We almost always have string cheese, shredded mozzarella, block mozzarella, and fresh mozzarella in our cheese drawer. It is lower in fat and calories than most cow's milk cheese, and has a simple, mild flavor that enhances almost any dish. This traditional pizza cheese works with casseroles, salads, quesadillas, tacos, and more. Mozzarella cheese is also a good source of phosphorus. Phosphorus aids in tooth formation, assists the body in utilizing other nutrients, and helps fight fatigue.

Parmigiano-reggiano cheese: Yes, I'm saying it again...I love this stuff, both as a healthnut and a foodie! Parmigiano-reggiano is a semi-hard cheese made from raw cow's milk in certain approved regions of Italy. It is typically aged 24 – 30 months. True Parmigiano-reggiano imparts an amazing rich flavor to many European inspired dishes. It is a pricey cheese, but a little goes a long way. Often just a couple of tablespoons as a garnish will be all you need. As a healthnut, I appreciate that Parmigiano-reggiano is easy to digest and great for people with gastrointestinal issues. In Italy, this cheese is often one of the first solid foods a baby eats, and is a great source of calcium. Do not confuse this with the stuff in the green shaker. That is a different product, and does not have the same health and flavor benefits of Parmigiano-reggiano.

Cherries: Cherries are hands down one of my favorite fruits. Unfortunately, they are constantly on Environmental Working Group's dirty dozen list, so source organic when available. Lucky for us, cherries freeze beautifully! When they peak in July and August, I buy bunches! I spend an afternoon pitting them, and then freeze them for smoothies, curries, and treats all year long. I end up spending a fraction of the cost of buying frozen organic cherries in December. Studies suggest that cherries are a natural pain reliever, help to reduce inflammation throughout the body, help fight cancer, can aid in weight loss, can help lower cholesterol, and help prevent memory loss. How are these little gems so powerful? Their dark color means that they are loaded with antioxidants and flavonoids! They also contain iron, vitamin C, magnesium, potassium, and beta carotene. Eat up, buttercup!

Chicken breasts with no added hormones or antibiotics, vegetarian fed: You might be surprised that I'm not trying to push you over to organic chicken breasts. While it is what I prefer, I understand chicken breasts are a common product and can be expensive when purchased as organic. Not everyone may want to splurge on them. What do I ask of you? PLEASE buy vegetarian fed chickens that have never been treated with hormones or antibiotics. When the hormones and antibiotics pass through the chickens, it absorbs into our soil, which in turn ends up in our drinking water and produce. This makes our bodies resistant to antibiotics when we truly need them and the added hormones have been shown to cause early puberty in young girls. Using vegetarian fed chicken is extremely important because animals are routinely fed animal by-products that are "unfit for human consumption". Hmm? They won't sell you the meat the chickens eat, but they will sell you the animals that ate this bad meat. Does that make any sense? Luckily, hormone and antibiotic free chicken is now available in many mainstream grocery stores (and Super Target!). It regularly goes on sale, so stock up when it does!

Chicken, as in the whole bird: When I started writing this cookbook, I thought there was no way I would ever roast a whole chicken. It sounded scary and well...scary. After watching my girls (and husband) gobble down my first succulent bird, I am a convert! I can get a whole hormone and antibiotic free five-pound chicken on sale for about $8.00. I can get an organic one for about $11.00. That is nuts! The first night, our family enjoys the roasted bird alongside simultaneously roasted vegetables. We shred the rest and store it in the freezer or fridge. The next time we have a recipe that calls for cooked chicken breasts, we just pull out our leftover chicken! You can also use the carcass to create homemade chicken stock. One carcass can yield two to three quarts of stock (which can also be frozen)! Why am I so passionate about hormone and antibiotic free chicken? Read the rant above under chicken breasts!

Organic chicken broth: Organic chicken broth (along with garlic and red onion) is the backbone of many of my recipes. I use it in everything! Whole Foods and Trader Joe's both sell it for $1.99/quart (may vary by date and region) and Costco usually carries it at a good price as well. The convenience it offers is well worth the money to me. It heightens the flavor of grains, and is a great alternative to additional oil or butter when sautéing veggies. I am devoted to buying this organically because broth is basically what is left when remaining chicken parts have been simmered for a very long time. It extracts the chicken flavor into the water. If conventional chickens have been fed animal by-products, hormones, and antibiotics, those are being extracted as well. I would prefer not to put that into my body.

Chicken sausage: What a great product! These come in a vast array of flavors and get dinner on the table in a snap. Being that they're made from chicken, they are naturally much lower in fat than pork sausage. Chicken sausage can usually be frozen in the package, making them a great product to keep on hand. Be sure to source brands that use vegetarian fed, hormone and antibiotic free chickens. My favorite brands include Applegate Farms, Lou's Famous, The Original Brat Haus, and Brooks Farms.

Boneless, skinless chicken thighs: Have I mentioned how important it is to source chicken thighs from hormone and antibiotic free chickens. If not, I'm saying it now. Dark chicken meat is higher in iron and B vitamins than white, and still has less fat than beef. It is also super tender, costs about $2.00/lb less than the breasts, and is super kid-friendly!

Organic chickpeas/garbanzo beans: Chickpeas are a popular food around the world. They are a cheap, tasty way to add meat-free protein, fiber, and nutrients to your diet. Chickpeas are thought to help your body detoxify the sulfites found in many processed foods and wine. I always try to buy organic beans because the cost difference is small. Adding just a cup or two of cooked beans is a great way to stretch your family's food dollar.

Chili powder: Here's the deal on chili powder. There is no official "recipe" for it. Brands can vary, so if you find one that you really love, stick with it. Chili powder is a blend of assorted dried chilies mixed with ingredients such as oregano, garlic, nutmeg, cumin, coriander, and pepper. Chili powder (like curry powder) offers a great spice base, but normally needs a bit of help from other, more pure spices, to take your dish in the direction you are going. Chili powder is a great addition to chili (duh), curries, Mexican and Indian dishes, and more. The capsaicin in the chilies offers immunity protection, is a natural anti-inflammatory, pain reliever, and promotes a healthy cardiovascular system. Flavor, health, and convenience in one little bottle?!? Nice.

Asian hot chili sauce: You may think that hot chili sauce is just another way to add heat and flavor to your dinner. In fact, it is way much more. (Can you believe that I just learned about this ingredient a year or two ago?!?) Those of us who love hot chili sauce most likely have small children or significant others with sensitive palates. Many of us also understand that the capsaicin in chilies can help rev the metabolism, fight inflammation, and boost the immune system. It is kind of a rock star. Hot chili sauce also allows us to prepare restaurant quality dishes that are toddler friendly, but lacking just one element...heat! Use often and use liberally!

Chipotle chili powder: Chipotle chili powder should not be confused with traditional chili powder. It is made from smoked and ground jalapeño peppers. (Read it this way: it is spicy!) If you use it in the increments that recipes call for chili powder, you will be creating an incredibly spicy, tear-inducing dish. (How do I know this? The first time I attempted baked beans, I substituted chipotle chili powder for the two tablespoons of traditional chili powder called for in my mom's recipe. Very...bad...idea.) Used in small increments, chipotle chili powder is awesome and adds a great smoky, spicy flavor to food. The health star in chipotle chili powder is capsaicin. Studies have shown that capsaicin helps relieve congestion, fight cancer, aid in weight loss, fight inflammation, and lower blood pressure.

Canned chipotle in adobo: The English translation of "chipotle in adobo" is, "smoked jalapeño peppers in sauce". (The Spanish version sure sounds sexier.) The "adobo" is usually a blend of Spanish spices, vinegar, garlic, tomatoes, and salt. These little suckers are spicy! Most recipes call for just one chipotle at a time. Luckily, I've come up with a way to keep you from wasting the rest of the can. Upon opening, puree the entire can. On a wax paper lined baking sheet, drop one-teaspoon increments of the puree. Transfer to freezer. When frozen, transfer little balls to a small freezer bag. One teaspoon of the puree is equal to approximately one chipotle. (Make it two, if you like it hot.) For information on the health benefits, read the above regarding "chipotle chili powder".

Chives: In addition to being a pretty garnish, chives are a great way to add a subtle, but not overpowering, flavor to more delicate dishes. As a member of the alluvium (onion, leek, garlic) family, chives offer many of the same health benefits without the pungent punch. Studies have shown that chives can aid in weight loss, prevent cancerous cells, and fight infection. (Did I mention they are really pretty, too?)

Cilantro: This is truly one of nature's miracle drugs. If you don't care for the taste of cilantro, please try it again. It naturally helps detoxify your body of heavy metals (found in many species of fish and packaged foods), is a natural anti-inflammatory, protects against salmonella poisoning, aids in digestion, and prevents nausea. It is also high in iron, magnesium, and many phytonutrients. There is a reason this is one of the worlds most popular and widely used herbs. Source organic when available.

Ground cinnamon: Cinnamon is another amazing, healing spice. It helps regulate blood sugar, helps lower LDL (bad) cholesterol, and is a natural food preservative. It also is a natural anti-inflammatory and can help increase mobility in arthritis patients. (I've experienced this personally.) Again, in the quantities used, it is worth paying the extra bit of money for the organic product.

Light coconut milk: Coconut milk is one of those foods that I think we will hear a lot more about in the near future. Scientists believe it has many healing abilities, but they are still trying to figure it out completely. What we do know is that it helps keep skin moist, is full of nutrients, and is a natural sweetener. Plus, it tastes good.

Shredded, unsweetened coconut: Recent studies have shown that the saturated fat in coconut is absorbed differently than the saturated fat in animals. It is incredibly healthful and has many medicinal properties. Around the world, coconut is used to give skin a healthy, youthful look (again with the vanity), prevent kidney stones, fight the flu and other viruses, prevent osteoporosis, stabilize blood sugar, and more. It gives chicken tenders a boost, and tastes great in cookies. Source unsweetened coconut, not the sweetened brands in the baking aisle.

Ground coriander: Coriander smells so good, filling the air when you cook with it. Plus, it's amazingly good for you! Coriander is the seed of the cilantro plant, so see my notes on "cilantro" above. It is available either ground or as dried seeds. I prefer the ground, as it gives the dish more flavor. Again, a little goes a long way, so invest in organic.

Fresh corn: Nothing says summer like fresh corn on the cob. Whether grilled, boiled, used in a salsa, or as part of a salad, fresh corn rocks. Please always source organic corn. Over 90% of the conventional corn grown in America is genetically modified. Often referred to as Franken foods, genetically modified (gmo) corn is laden with chemicals and pesticides. It has been linked to third generation infertility, and has been banned in the European Union. Introduced in 1996, genetically modified corn and soy are so new to the market that no one understands the long term affect these foods will have on humans. (The same is true for tofu, edamame, and canola oil.) Don't let big agriculture play Russian roulette with your health. As more research unfolds, the dangers of these foods are becoming more and more transparent.

Frozen organic corn: This is one of my favorite frozen products. With all of the talk about BPA in can liners, I decided to make the switch. You know what? It tastes better and is just as easy to use. Corn is one of the most genetically modified products out there, so PLEASE always go organic or gmo-free. (See "fresh corn" for more information on gmo's.) Corn is a great, inexpensive way to add bulk to foods and also offers a pretty color. It is also full of niacin, folate, and fiber.

Corn starch: Corn starch is used as a thickening agent for many broth based soups and sauces. It is literally the starch of the corn. When researching this ingredient, I was surprised to find that some people believe that eating large amounts of corn starch carries health risks. When I looked into it further, I realized that these people were consuming multiple boxes of corn starch a week. I have concluded that using small amounts to thicken healthy, healing soups, marinades, and stir-fries should not have any adverse effects on your health. What is important? Sourcing brands of corn starch that use non-gmo corn. See above rant on "fresh corn".

Whole wheat couscous: Whole wheat couscous is a great source of whole grains and it can be ready in 10 minutes (including the time it takes to heat the broth). It adds a great nutty flavor to a variety of dishes, and supplies the body with about 60% more nutrients than the non-whole wheat variety (including B vitamins, folic acid, iron, and fiber).

Crabmeat: Crab just makes a meal feel special. I'm so jealous of all you northeasterners who get to indulge on it regularly! Crab is a smaller sea creature, so it is lower in mercury than larger species. It is chock full of omega-3 fatty acids, supports a healthy immune system, and is high in protein.

Crushed red pepper flakes: We all know that crushed red pepper flakes are a great way to add heat to a dish. What you may not know is that the capsaicin in red pepper is a natural anti-inflammatory, boosts the metabolism, and can improve your mood. If you can handle the heat, you will burn more calories, be happier, and be healthier just by upping your use of this simple spice. That's hot!

Cucumber: I love cucumber. Its high water content and crispy crunch is so satisfying. Technically a fruit, this summer sensation contains vitamin C and silica (a crucial nutrient for glowing skin). Pregnant? Eat more cucumber! It will help reduce puffiness and bloating from the inside out. One cup of this jewel contains just 15 calories, making them a great way to bulk a dish up without bulking you up! Wondering whether to peel or not to peel? If you buy your cucumbers organically or wax free, eat your skins. Many of the cucumbers nutrients are concentrated just under the skin. If you buy conventionally produced cucumbers, I would suggest peeling them. Many of the waxes used on cucumbers are petroleum based. I doubt that petroleum is something you want to be feeding yourself or your family.

Ground cumin: Cumin is another one of the amazing super spices! It boosts the immune system, aids in digestion, and is even thought to have a detoxifying affect on cancer patients. It is also a great spice for new mommies who are struggling with milk production. Cumin is a natural way to increase milk supply!

Mild curry powder: I love mild curry powder for its ability to give excellent flavor to an otherwise simple dish. Curry powder is a blend of India's most healing spices, including turmeric, cumin, coriander, ginger, fenugreek, nutmeg, fennel, cinnamon, white pepper, cardamom, cloves, and cayenne. I'll make my own taco seasoning, but not my own curry powder!

D

E

Organic, free range eggs: Organic, free range eggs are one of the most affordable organic protein sources available. The chickens are humanely raised without any hormones or antibiotics, are given access to omega-3 rich grasses, and are higher in vital nutrients choline (which reduces inflammation) and lutein (which helps prevent eye degeneration as you age). It was once believed that the cholesterol in eggs resulted in higher levels of cholesterol in humans; this is no longer an accepted fact. Eggs are a great addition to any diet.

Heirloom eggplant: The beauty of eggplant is its ability to take on the flavor of any pairing. I use heirloom (smaller) eggplant because you don't have to "sweat out" the bitterness like you do with the big ones. They are super kid-friendly, low in calories, and a good source of magnesium, copper, and potassium. Studies suggest that eating eggplant can provide relief to achy joints. They also fight the cells that cause cancer and contain anti-viral agents.

Egg noodles: Egg noodles are basically traditional noodles that incorporate up to 20% egg into the dough. In addition to the added protein and lutein, egg noodles have a thicker consistency than traditional noodles. I love to use them as a base for very simple noodle dishes.

F

Fennel: I think fennel is phenomenal. As a person who has suffered from inflammation and a damaged immune system, I try to eat fennel often. I like it raw, roasted and sautéed. I like the flavor the seeds impart as well. Fennel contains a powerful phytonutrient called anethole. Research has shown that anethole acts as a TNF-blocker, a powerful drug that fights inflammation, cancer, and promotes a healthy immune system. Often used in French and Italian cooking, fennel is quickly gaining popularity in the U.S. When purchasing fennel, look for firm, moist, bulbs. Bulbs that are beginning to shrivel or brown will be less flavorful than the fresher ones.

Ground fennel: When you add ground fennel to a dish, your fellow diners will definitely be trying to pin point the flavor. When you tell them what it is, you will probably hear a lot of "ah-has". Ground fennel is just that, fennel seeds ground into a powder. Popular in European cooking, fennel seeds are what give Italian sausage its unique flavor. They also help fight indigestion, tummy woes, and bloating. Supposedly, if you swallow a pinch of the powder, it is even more effective than the yucky pink stuff!

Fish sauce: Ingredients: Anchovy extract, salt, sugar. Fish sauce is weird. On its own, it is not very tasty. Combined with other traditional Thai ingredients, it rocks! Many people swear by using anchovy extract in their cooking. They say it takes a dish to a level that no other ingredient can. I've not yet used anchovies in any form other than fish sauce, but it really works in this form. Anchovies are a great source of protein, omega-3's, and calcium. Studies have shown that they can help to reduce cholesterol, are low in mercury, and promote a healthy heart.

Unbleached all-purpose flour: Wow! I've been using unbleached flour for years, but I was never really sure why. I assumed that bleaching the wheat stripped away the vital nutrients, minerals, and fiber that are important for good health. What I found out is so much more. According to the research, bleached flour is often bleached with chlorine, bromates, and peroxides. All three are banned as a bleaching agent in the European Union. That made me curious. It turns out that bromates are a carcinogen that has caused recalls in drinking water, including the Dasani recall in Europe, and the draining of the Silver Lake reservoir by the Los Angeles Department of Water and Power. In addition, 50% to 80% of the nutrients in wheat are lost during the bleaching process. You don't believe me? "Enriched bleached flour" is one of the most common ingredients in processed foods. During the bleaching process, so many nutrients have been stripped away that the FDA has required that cheap, synthetic versions of the wheat's natural nutrients are added. Save yourself the problems, and go unbleached all the way!

White whole wheat flour: White whole wheat flour is one of my favorite flours for just about anything. It is made from hard white wheat, as opposed to hard red winter wheat. This gives it a lighter texture, color, and flavor while still offering a heaping portion of whole grains. White whole wheat has been popular in Europe for centuries. It is just as nutritious as red wheat, but with a more mild, sweet flavor. It is also less dense. White whole wheat is a good source of manganese, B vitamins, iron, and magnesium. Regularly consuming whole grains can help you maintain a stable blood sugar level and a healthy weight.

Whole wheat flour: Whole wheat flour is a rich, nutty, chewy, and dense delicacy. A dense loaf of properly prepared baked whole wheat bread is heavenly. Unfortunately, most people still associate 100% whole wheat with dry and dismal. Please try again. According to the Mayo Clinic, whole grains are considered the "staff of life". Studies have shown that whole wheat provides fiber, protein, fights insulin resistance, lowers cholesterol, prevents diabetes, and helps to prevent metabolic syndrome.

Fuji apples: An apple a day keeps the doctor away? Maybe. Apples contain antioxidants, flavonoids, and fiber that promote a healthy heart and lungs, fight asthma and cancer, and support a healthy cardiovascular system. The pectin in apples can assist with irritable bowel system and other tummy troubles. Apples are consistently on Environmental Working Group's dirty dozen list, so please be sure to source organic whenever possible.

G

Garam Masala: "Hot spice" is the English translation of "garam masala". I find that interesting, since it really isn't a spicy mixture. The combination of spices can vary from brand to brand, but they all add an unusual complexity of flavors that would be difficult to duplicate at home (without spending money on spices that you may not use up). I've found that just a bit of this spice blend can totally give curries the "hmm..." factor. Some of the spices used in garam masala can include coriander, fennel, black peppercorns, cardamom, nutmeg, caraway, ginger, cloves, kalonji (?!?), cassia cinnamon, star anise, cumin, Malabar leaves, and/or bay leaves. Someday, I may tackle it. For now, I will just buy the jar. (I get mine from Penzeys Spices.)

Garlic: "How do I love thee, let me count the ways." The "stinking rose" is my all-time favorite smell, and (along with onions) is the one herb I could not cook without. It adds aroma and flavor to any dish, and its sweet yet hot flavor is impossible to recreate. It is a natural immunity booster, and has long been praised in Eastern medicine for its medicinal qualities. I try to eat garlic everyday. It has been shown to help reduce free radicals in the bloodstream, and is beneficial to pretty much every system in the body. Eat it. Often.

Garlic powder: Some days you want a shortcut, some days you just want to make sure that every bite of your meal is infused with flavor. Garlic powder delivers both. It is important that you only buy the amount that you can consume within six months, and that you seek organic whenever possible. Supposedly, ¼ tsp of garlic powder is equal to 2 cloves of fresh garlic. As far as the health benefits, look one slot above. Garlic powder (while slightly less medicinal) offers most of the same benefits mentioned in fresh garlic.

Garlic salt: As a tween (yes, I just used that word), one of the first "recipes" I created was garlic noodles. It was, quite simply, spaghetti tossed in butter and seasoned with garlic salt. I am filled with mixed emotions as I admit that this is still one of my favorite foods (eaten with an array of sautéed vegetables, of course...or not). All of this to say, garlic salt is a great way to add an amazing dimension of flavor to the most simple of ingredients. It is a combination of garlic, salt, and sometimes parsley. Garlic rules. I love it. Learn more by reading the "garlic" rant above.

Fresh ginger: Ginger is another one of those amazingly flavorful, medicinal foods that I absolutely adore from both a healthnut and foodie perspective. When I was suffering from morning sickness, I snacked on crystallized ginger and drank real ginger ale throughout the day. It was the only thing that could relieve my nausea. It also is known to aid in digestion by helping to break down the fatty acids and proteins in foods. Ground ginger has a completely different flavor profile than fresh. Store remaining fresh ginger in the freezer wrapped tightly in saran wrap and then in a freezer bag. Use a sharp knife or microplane to cut off just the amount needed. Ground ginger (3:1, fresh to ground) or crushed ginger (1:1) can always be substituted for fresh, but the flavor will not be quite as bright, and the medicinal qualities not as strong.

Ground ginger: The flavors of ground ginger are so different from fresh ginger, that it is silly! Ground ginger is much more musty and pungent than fresh. It is also a great way of infusing an entire dish with flavor, as opposed to offering flavor "blasts" from the fresh. Whether you enjoy it powdered or fresh, ginger is full of medicinal properties. Studies have shown that ginger can help prevent migraines, menstrual cramps, and heartburn. It can also help regulate the digestive tract, reduce blood pressure, and prevent diabetes.

Pickled ginger: Pickled ginger has long been a staple on any plate of sushi. My friend, Izzy, introduced it to me as an addition to her Asian crab and noodle salad (recipe on my blog). I looked into the different options available and realized that it can be very healthful **IF** you make sure to avoid versions that contain high fructose corn syrup and red no. 40. The ingredients in naturally pickled ginger are **ginger, rice vinegar, sugar,** and **salt.** Please source only brands that are made in this way. Natural pickled ginger will develop a pink hue as it ages; it will not be bright pink.

Grapes: Who doesn't like grapes? Good and good for you, grapes contain flavonoids, phenolic acids, and resveratrol. Studies have shown that these phytonutrients can lower your risk for stroke, high blood pressure, heart disease, and cancer. As with wine, red and purple grapes offer more protection than green. Currently, imported grapes are number 12 on the Environmental Working Group's dirty dozen list. If you cannot find or afford organic grapes, try to source grapes grown in the USA. They tend to contain fewer pesticides than ones grown abroad.

Greek yogurt, 2%: According to Grecian folklore, yogurt is a natural aphrodisiac. If that isn't enough, it is full of probiotics, and a lower fat and calorie alternative to cream or mayonnaise. Probiotics strengthen your immune system and help ward off disease and infections. Studies also suggest that consuming three servings of low-fat dairy a day will help you lose almost 25% more weight than diet alone.

Green beans: Vitamin K is a nutrient that most Americans are deficient in. According to many holistic practitioners, vitamin K is expected to be the next vitamin D! Just one cup of green beans offers about 25% of your daily needs. Vitamin K is crucial for bone strength, and reduces your chance of developing cancer or diabetes. Green beans also offer manganese, potassium, and magnesium.

Canned green chilies: Canned green chilies are most often made from Anaheim chili peppers. Diced green chilies add a subtle, smoky heat to Southwest and Hispanic dishes. Studies have shown that eating green chilies can help to reduce blood pressure, fight migraines, boost the metabolism, and reduce inflammation.

Green enchilada sauce: Green enchilada sauce is one of the few things that I still buy in a can. It is entirely possible to make your own, but the process of roasting green chilies, peppers, and tomatillos is definitely time consuming. The ingredients in green enchilada sauce boost your immunity (vitamin C), revs the metabolism (capsaicin), and help repair cell damage from the exposure to everyday toxins (antioxidants). Be sure to read the ingredients on the labels! Some brands sneak in high fructose corn syrup or MSG (monosodium glutamate).

Green onions: Like other onions, green onions (or scallions or spring onions) are great way to boost your immune system. In Chinese medicine, green onions are used to fight off the common cold, and are believed to have anti-bacterial and anti-fungal properties. I love the subtle spice they give to a dish and that they can be eaten raw. I also think they make a pretty garnish!

Mixed greens: When researching the health benefits of salad greens, I was reminded over and over again that many of the largest and strongest mammals on the Earth sustain primarily on greens. That blew my mind and made me dig even deeper. I've realized that "man" could probably sustain on greens alone. After all, 100% grass-fed cows do, and look how big and strong they are! When sourcing greens, it is best if you eat a variety. This is the reason that I usually call for mixed greens in many of my salads. Please remember that many of the nutrients in

greens are fat-soluble. This is why I always dress them in healthy oil.
Pig out and enjoy!

H

Wild caught halibut: Halibut is hands down my absolute favorite fish to eat. It has a firm, flaky texture, mildly sweet flavor, and delicate, yet hearty (I know) texture. Lucky for me, it is also one of the top fish nutritionally. One 6-ounce serving of halibut provides your body with over 25% of its daily needs of tryptophan, selenium, protein, omega-3, niacin, phosphorus, magnesium, vitamin B6, and vitamin B12. To save a few dollars, I buy our fish frozen and defrost it at home. Feeding your family wild, sustainable fish at home is a great way to satisfy cravings for delicious food, while simultaneously healing and nourishing our bodies from the inside out. (I totally want halibut for dinner now...)

Herbs de Provence: Herbs de Provence is as varied of a spice blend as there are cooks in France. However, it is one of those blends that I love. We know that herbs and spices are flavorful and healing. Some nights you just need something to sprinkle into your pasta or sauce. It may not be the perfect combination of flavors, but it is easy, healthful, and lends great flavors to French, Italian, and American dishes alike. I may even try it with Mexican soon. Basil, marjoram, savory, thyme, rosemary, oregano, and mint are all common players.

Hoisin sauce: Hoisin sauce is a sweet and spicy soy-based sauce that is often used in traditional Asian cooking. Like fish sauce, hoisin is one of those rare Asian combinations that works great, but is hard to describe. If you've ever had moo-shu at a Chinese restaurant, you know the flavor of hoisin sauce. As a general rule, brands imported from China will taste better (and more authentic) than ones created elsewhere.

Hominy: Hominy is corn that has had the germ removed. When boiled, it puffs up (for lack of a better description) and has a great chewy texture that is ready to absorb whatever flavor you add to it. Also called posole, hominy is popular in Mexican, Southern, and Southwestern dishes. You may not be familiar with hominy, but I bet that you've heard of grits. Grits are the ground and dried product of hominy.

Raw honey: Besides being sweet and tasting great in hot drinks, honey offers amazing health benefits! It is a natural immunity booster, can be tolerated by many people with diabetes, helps cure upper respiratory infections, and can be used topically to treat burns. It is touted worldwide for its medicinal properties, especially when enjoyed with vinegar. DO NOT give raw honey (or any honey) to babies under a year.

They can develop botulism. Botulism is a rare, but possibly fatal disease that can cause muscle weakness and paralysis. This is the only food that Annie and Ellie did not eat before 15 months. I gave them all of the common allergens, but no honey!

Hummus: Hummus is a Middle Eastern dip or spread that is made from chickpeas, olive oil, lemon juice, and garlic. It is available in a variety of flavors. Chickpeas (as all beans) are digested slowly, making them a great staple for people who suffer from diabetes or insulin resistance. (I've struggled with insulin resistance for years, so I eat hummus all the time!) The monounsaturated fats in olive oil offer just enough healthy fat to help your body properly absorb the vegetables you are serving it with. When purchasing store bought hummus, be sure to read the label! Many brands swap genetically modified canola or vegetable oil for the heart healthy olive oil. Yuck!

I

Salt free Italian seasoning: Salt free Italian seasoning is a combination of many popular Italian spices, including basil, sage, rosemary, marjoram, oregano, and/or thyme. It is a great blend of healing herbs and spices that taste great sprinkled onto veggies, chicken, or pastas.

J

K

Kalamata olives: A staple in Mediterranean cooking, olives have been praised and consumed for centuries. They are full of healthy monounsaturated and polyunsaturated fats, and add a nice meaty texture to many recipes. They taste great thrown into a salad or pasta, and make a great topping for bruschetta and pizza. Properly refrigerated after opening, they have a long shelf life so they are easy to keep on hand.

L

No-bake lasagna noodles: No-bake lasagna noodles are the fancy shmancy noodles that don't have to be boiled ahead of time. (They rock.) According to manufacturers, the only difference between no-bake and traditional lasagna noodles is the fact that the no-bake noodles are thinner. That means you can soften the noodles using only the sauce and other healthy ingredients that you pack into your lasagna. If you use traditional lasagna noodles, you will need to boil them ahead of time. For nutrient information, please read "organic pasta".

Leeks: Now that I understand the proper way to prepare leeks, I love them! They make a good alternative to onions, offering a more subtle flavor, while still providing many of the same health benefits. Leeks help to stabilize blood sugar, lower bad cholesterol, and raise good cholesterol at the same time! Sounds good to me!

Lemon juice: I love lemon juice! (I know, I say that about a lot of things. It makes me glad that our relationship with ingredients doesn't have to be a monogamous one!) Lemon juice is a virtually calorie free way to add tang and flavor to any dish. Lemons are also incredibly good for you. They are packed with phytonutrients and vitamin C. Lemon juice is a natural diuretic and can help relieve both nausea and constipation. It is also a natural immunity booster and helps ward off cancer. Amazing.

Lemon zest: Adding lemon zest to a dressing or dish really builds another layer of flavor. The zest of a lemon refers to just the bright shiny, yellow skin. Once that is removed, you are left with the pith, which is not as flavorful. The zest of a lemon is full of healthy oils that leach into a dish as it cooks or marinades. The easiest way to zest a lemon is to use a tool called a microplane or a zester. They can be found at any shop you would buy cooking utensils (Bed Bath & Beyond, Williams Sonoma, Sur la Table, Target, etc).

Lentils: These are a great fast cooking alternative to beans. Alone, lentils don't have much flavor, but they soak up whatever ingredients you combine them with. They are rich in protein, fiber, iron, magnesium, and folate. Studies have shown that lentils help stabilize blood sugar, lower cholesterol, and prevent heart disease.

Lime juice: Limes are packed with vitamin C, making them a great immunity booster! They (and all citrus fruits) are a great food to eat when fighting a bug. Limes also have anti-carcinogenic properties, making them the perfect thing to serve over charred steak. I squeeze a half a lime into sparkling water almost every afternoon to keep illness at bay! (My Costco sells huge bags for $4.00.)

Lime zest: Adding lime zest to a dressing or dish really builds another layer of flavor. The zest of the lime refers to bright shiny green skin. Once that is removed, you are left with the pith, which is not as flavorful. The zest of a lime is full of healthy oils that leach into a dish as it cooks or marinades. The easiest way to zest a lime is to use a tool called a microplane or a zester. They can be found at any shop you would buy cooking utensils. (Yes, just like "lemon zest".)

M

Mandarin oranges: I buy these in a can. If you are up for it (and if they are available), you can purchase Mandarin oranges and segment them yourself. However, on the times that I pop open a can of these tasty gems, it is because I need fruit now! I always source the brands that are packed in juice (not syrup), and I love to keep them around for those days that our fresh fruit supply has dwindled.

Mangoes: We eat a ton of mangoes, and we spend very little money on them. A few times a year, mangoes go on sale for 50 or 60 cents a piece. When they do, I buy tons! Mangoes are a dense fruit that freeze beautifully. Unlike berries, frozen mangoes taste just as great as fresh when gently defrosted in the refrigerator. Mangoes are nutritional superstars as well. They provide iron, vitamin C, and beta carotene. Mangoes give your immune system a boost, fight off infection, and are a great source of energy.

Manicotti shells: Manicotti shells are pasta tubes that are stuffed, and then baked with a sauce. Most recipes require you to parboil the shells before stuffing. I've found that if you use enough sauce, you can skip that step altogether. For more information on nutrition, see "organic pasta".

Pure maple syrup: Please only use real maple syrup!!! The "maple flavored" varieties are just that, high fructose corn syrup and artificial flavors. The "no added sugar" kinds are full of chemically derived artificial sweeteners. You may save a couple dollars now, but your health pays for it down the road. Pure maple syrup is the sap of a maple tree. It contains antioxidants, including manganese and zinc. Used in moderation, it is a great addition to the diet, and adds a great flavor to dips, sauces, and marinades.

Marsala wine: Marsala wine is a sweet Italian wine produced in the region of Marsala, located in the southern most part of Italy. Similar to port, but a lot more affordable, Marsala wine is popular for the way it infuses a sweet and savory flavor to a variety of cuisines. When stored in a cool dark space (not above the stove), Marsala lasts for many months. If unavailable, Madiera wine makes a suitable substitute.

Mayonnaise: Sometimes, you just need mayo. Real mayo. I've got to tell you, when I'm going to use it, I always go full fat. When used sparingly, mayonnaise adds a great tangy flavor to a dressing, sauce, or dip. When purchasing mayonnaise, remember that the shorter the ingredient list, the better. Traditionally, mayonnaise requires just three ingredients: olive oil, egg yolks, and lemon juice (or vinegar). Obviously, the ones you buy in the store will have a few additions. Be sure to read labels and to avoid brands that use inferior oils or high fructose corn syrup.

Organic, whole milk: After speaking with multiple dairy farmers and doing large amounts of research, I have decided to feed my family organic whole milk, not skim or low-fat. Here's why... When you skim the fat off the top of the milk, you are left with a bunch of sugar that is confused about what it should be doing. In whole milk, the fat, protein, and carbohydrates work together to build bones, brain cells, and can help prevent metabolic syndrome. If available, source milk from a local dairy that allows their cows to pasture feed (eat grass), are hormone free, and use reusable glass bottles. This will boost the nutrients in your milk even more. It will also ensure that the chemicals in the plastic or cardboard containers are not leaching into your milk, and then into your body. (Plus, grass-fed milk is naturally leaner, tastes better, and the glass bottles are better for the environment!)

Baby bella/Cremini mushrooms: After much research, I've realized that these two varieties of mushrooms are one in the same. Cremini and baby bella mushrooms are incredibly high in phytonutrients, and are an incredible cancer fighting agent. They are also rich in vitamin B2 (an energy booster), zinc (an immunity booster), and riboflavin (which fights migraines). Mushrooms add a great meaty texture to dishes. This allows you to save money and calories, while still enjoying a large portion of food!

Shitake mushrooms: Another one of those great medicinal foods used in Chinese medicine, shitake mushrooms are thought to increase life expectancy. Whether or not that is true, we do know that shitake mushrooms are a great source of iron, vitamin C, and fiber. They are also an immunity booster and can help lower cholesterol.

White mushrooms: The more I research mushrooms, the more I fall in love with them. They are virtually calorie free, making them a great choice for people trying to maintain a healthy weight. Eastern culture has long praised them for their medicinal benefits. Vegetarians love them for their ability to stand in for meat. I love them because they taste great, are inexpensive, and are high in healing nutrients.

Mushrooms have more potassium per gram than bananas, help rev up the metabolism, and are great at fighting cancer cells!

Coarse ground (Creole) mustard: This is one of those ingredients that make food taste amazing. The whole mustard seed is included, so it is also incredibly rich in nutrients. Whole grain mustard is an amazing way to add flavor and nutrients to almost any dish. It works in dressings, aioli, pork rubs, whatever. It helps boost the metabolism, fight disease, and lower high blood pressure.

Dijon mustard: Dijon mustard is another one of my go-to ingredients in the kitchen. I add it to vinaigrettes, remoulades, vegetables, proteins, beans, soups, and the list goes on. It is an inexpensive, low-calorie, and healthy way to add a burst of extra flavor to a variety of dishes. Mustard seeds are also high in selenium and magnesium. These minerals have been shown to give relief to asthma patients, lower blood pressure, and help regulate sleep patterns.

Dry/ground/powdered mustard: Mustard powder is just that, dried yellow (or brown) mustard seeds that are ground into a powder. It is very versatile, and adds a great depth of flavor without the added acidity in prepared mustard. Powdered mustard is more pungent than the prepared version, so the medicinal benefits run deep. Mustard seeds are rich in phytonutrients and can help prevent cancer cells from developing. Consuming them can also help reduce inflammation in the body and the severity of asthma.

Yellow mustard seeds: Mustard seeds are holistic rock stars! They are naturally antibacterial, boost the metabolism, help prevent migraines, and reduce inflammation. They also promote a healthy immune system. They are basically a calorie free way to add nutrients and flavor to any dish! Nice.

N

Farfalle noodles: Farfalle is the name given to the type of pasta that looks like bow ties (or hair bows if you have a little princess). If Farfalle is unavailable, suitable substitutions include fusilli (corkscrew), pipe rigate, wagon wheels, penne, or small shells. You want a noodle that will allow the sauce and other ingredients to mingle with the noodles, not just be ladled on top. For nutrition information, see "organic pasta".

Linguine noodles: Linguine noodles are a cross between spaghetti and fettuccine. Either one would make a suitable substitution. For nutrition information, see "organic pasta".

Orecchiette noodles: Orecchiette are "little pig ear" shaped pasta. Annie loves it anytime we have "piggy pasta" for lunch or dinner. If orecchiette is unavailable, you may substitute small shells. Orecchiette originated with Italian chefs that used their thumb prints to flatten the little ball of pasta dough. (I think I may have to try this!) For nutrition information, see "organic pasta".

Pipe rigate noodles: I love pipe rigate noodles for their fun, curly shape, and for all of the bulk it adds to a recipe. A serving of pipe rigate looks like so much more than a serving of spaghetti! If you cannot find pipe rigate, you can replace it with penne, ziti, shells, elbows, or fusilli (any airy pasta shape). For nutrition information, see "organic pasta".

Rice noodles: Do not confuse traditional Asian rice noodles with brown rice noodles. True rice noodles are made from white rice flour and water. Brown rice noodles are a gluten-free alternative to traditional noodles. Normally, I am against white flour and rice; however, for a traditional pad Thai, you must use this ingredient. The recipes I use rice noodles in are so high in other forms of fiber, vitamins, and minerals that I am not worried. Are rice noodles packed full of healing nutrients? No. Used in moderation, can they be part of a healing, healthy meal? Yes.

Spaghetti noodles: I really don't think this ingredient needs much of an explanation. Growing up, we ate spaghetti noodles with jarred tomato sauce, Italian bread, and salad at least once a week. I guess it was my mom's version of Meat free Monday before it was trendy! Angel hair, linguine, and fettuccine all make suitable substitutes. See "organic pasta" for nutrition information.

Nutmeg: Nutmeg is one of those flavors that make you go "hmm". I still don't know quite how to describe it. I do know that studies have shown that nutmeg is a natural anti-inflammatory, revs up the metabolism, detoxifies the liver and kidneys, and aids stomach woes. Oh yes, technically, nutmeg is a seed.

O

Extra virgin olive oil: Extra virgin olive oil is one of the best ways to counteract the negative effects of the processed American diet. It is rich in monounsaturated fatty acids, omega-3 fatty acids, and omega-9 fatty acids. If you look at counties where a lot of olive oil is used in cooking, you will see that the people have much lower amounts of chronic disease than Americans. I try to make olive oil a staple in our daily diet.

Red onion: While all onions are healthy, red onions top the chart! Their vibrant purple color indicates that they have higher levels of antioxidants than the paler varieties. This may sound odd, but I think that onions might be the vegetable my girls eat most. Once they've spent a few minutes sweating in the skillet, onions offer a sweet, subtle flavor that can enhance just about any dish. They are virtually calorie free, and are a great way to add bulk and health benefits to a simple meal. Onions can help lower bad (LDL) cholesterol, fight off infection, and reduce the severity of asthma. Topping Environmental Working Group's Clean 15 list, you may be happy to know that it is not crucial to source them organically. When I got interested in holistic eating, onions were one of the first foods I began piling into my body. I think they are very medicinal, and I do my best to make sure my family eats them several times a week.

Yellow onion: Yellow onions have a stronger flavor than red onions. They are the traditional choice in Indian cooking and work well in lighter colored dishes and soups. While slightly lower in antioxidants than my beloved red onions, yellow onions are still a great immunity booster, help to lower LDL (bad) cholesterol, and can help to lower blood pressure.

Orange juice: Not only is orange juice a tasty breakfast drink, it also tastes amazing in sauces, dips, and salad dressings! Orange juice is a great way to give your immune system a boost, fight off the common cold, reduce inflammation, and even reduce cholesterol. It is high in phytonutrients, vitamin C, and folic acid.

Dried oregano: Oregano is a spice that I love to use. I often find it hard to finish a whole package of fresh sprigs before they spoil, so I often turn to dried. It has all of the same medicinal properties as fresh (see directly below), and gives a great flavor to many dishes. In a pinch, you may substitute one teaspoon of dried oregano for every one tablespoon of fresh oregano a recipe calls for.

Fresh oregano: Native to Greece, oregano is translated "joy of the mountain". It gets its flavor from spending lots of time basking in the hot sun. This makes it great for growing in summer home gardens. Oregano pairs beautifully with tomatoes, and is rich in healing, medicinal properties. Oregano is a good source of vitamins K, A, and C, calcium, iron, and manganese. It can help lower cholesterol, reduce the formation of cancer cells, and is a natural anti-bacterial. If you have fresh oregano on hand, feel free to substitute one tablespoon of the fresh leaves for every 1 tsp of dried oregano called for in a recipe.

Mexican oregano: While Greek (or Mediterranean) oregano is related to mint, Mexican oregano is related to lemon verbena. They have similar undertones, but Mexican oregano is a bit brighter and more citrus-y. It pairs especially well with cumin, smoked paprika, and tomatoes. Using the Mexican variety does make a difference (when called for), and is available at many large supermarket chains.

Orzo: Orzo is a Mediterranean type of pasta that is about the same size as cooked rice. It is a nice addition to soups, risottos, and pilafs. Orzo is easy to find in your local market, and is a fun, kid-friendly ingredient to cook with. For nutrition information, see "organic pasta".

P

Smoked paprika: Also called Spanish paprika, this smoky spice is a great way to add a rich, smoky flavor without adding fat. It is nothing like the paprika your mom used to sprinkle over deviled eggs. It is traditionally made from dried peppers that have been smoked in oak. Smoked paprika can help normalize blood pressure, fight infection, and boost immunity.

Sweet (Hungarian) paprika: Sweet paprika is a nice blend of sweet and spicy peppers. Don't worry, sweet paprika is not hot, it just adds a subtle undertone (and a pretty color) to a dish. By allowing the peppers to spend lots of time in the hot sunshine, they naturally sweeten. Paprika is rich in vitamin C, has antibacterial properties, and aids in digestion.

Flat leaf parsley: Did you know that two tablespoons of parsley provides over 150% of your vitamin K needs?!? As scientists are realize that vitamin K is crucial for healthy bones, this is an important fact. Thanks to a volatile oil called myristicin, parsley can help reduce your absorption of certain carcinogens found in grilled food and cigarettes. Next time you grill, add some parsley to your plate or marinade!

Jarred pasta sauce: Though I dream of the day that I have nothing to do but simmer an organic blend of fresh tomatoes, herbs, and spices for hours, today, I am thankful for the amazing array of tasty, organic jarred sauces that are now widely available. I've also come to the conclusion that it is probably healthier to use jarred sauces (packaged in glass), than to make your own from canned tomatoes (chemicals in the can lining). You may have to shop around a little bit to find a brand you love, but when you do, stock up! (My personal favorite is Trader Joe's tomato and basil)

Organic pasta: I'm often asked what type of pasta I feed my family. People are often surprised (and relieved) when I answer, "organic pasta". "Not whole wheat?" they ask excitedly. Nope. I have never found a whole wheat brand that can offer the satisfaction I expect from a pasta dinner. I do love organic pasta, and consider it a close second. Made from hard durum wheat semolina, organic pasta is one of my key tricks to creating restaurant quality meals at home. Organic noodles are cut using a traditional artisan bronze cut method. This leaves the noodles with ridged edges, allowing the sauce to more easily cling to the noodle. Because it is fast and less expensive, most conventional brands of pasta are cut using chemically heavy Teflon dyes. This is why conventional noodles have a smoother finish and more yellow color. By using organic pasta, you will not only be able to avoid the dangers of the Teflon dyes, you will also know that your wheat was raised without the use of synthetic fertilizers and pesticides. Your finished noodle will be just a noodle, unbleached and free from preservatives, additives, or other cheap fillers. As a foodie, I think that organic pasta tastes amazing! It is made in the "old world" style, and has a great nutty flavor that makes me feel as though I am enjoying a dish with my (wistfully imagined) Italian ancestors.

Organic peaches: Peaches are another food consistently listed on the Environmental Working Group's dirty dozen list. When available, please source the organic variety. Ripe peaches are a great first finger food for babies and are packed full of phytonutrients, potassium, and vitamin C. They can help boost the immune system, lower cholesterol, and fight the cells that can cause cancer.

Organic peanuts: I always buy peanuts organically. If you track the increase in peanut allergies, you will notice that it has risen in similar proportions to the increase in the pesticides use on conventional peanuts. Maybe it's the pesticides, not the peanuts. Peanuts are high in antioxidants, healthy monounsaturated fat, and resveratrol (the stuff in wine that helps protect the heart). Peanuts also make a great on-the-go snack for big and little kids alike. (Because peanuts are a choking hazard, they are not meant for babies.) I almost always have a small container of peanuts (or almonds) and raisins in my bag for emergency hunger attacks.

Organic peanut butter: This might be one of the best foods ever! It is an inexpensive and tasty way to fuel your body with protein, heart-healthy fats, and fiber. Again, please buy the organic version. Many of the brands we grew up eating, now contain high fructose corn syrup and hydrogenated oils. Organic peanut butter contains roasted organic peanuts, and maybe salt. We love peanut butter in smoothies, oatmeal, noodle dishes, fruit dip, "quesadillas", and "sushi" rolls; the possibilities are endless. (Darren has even tried peanut butter on a hamburger after seeing it on Diners, Drive-ins, and Dives.)

Pecans: First off, pecans taste amazing! Mixed with mushrooms or lentils, topped on salads, or crusting a fish, pecans are delicious. Even better, they have more antioxidants per ounce than almost any other popular nut. They are rich in vitamin E, omega-3 fatty acids, and polyunsaturated fat (one of the healthy kinds). Alone or mixed with dried fruit, pecans are a great way to keep you satiated on the go. Studies also suggest that a daily one-ounce serving of nuts can help prevent weight gain or aid in weight loss. Fat is no longer the enemy.

Frozen peas: This is one ingredient I always have in my freezer. Inexpensive, nutritious, and easy to prepare, we love frozen peas! They have a sweet, neutral flavor than can add bulk to almost any dish. Did you know that one cup of green peas offers between 10% to over 50% of 18 different vitamins and minerals?!? That's a lot. As far as health benefits, peas are a natural way to detoxify the body from the toxins we are exposed to everyday. They help promote a healthy heart, and help fight off infection, cancer, and anemia. After learning all this, I'm so glad we had peas for dinner tonight (Pork Vindaloo).

Pepitas: Pepita is the Mexican term for little pumpkin seeds. I love to eat them roasted and salted as a snack, or as a way to enhance my cooking. They have a great flavor, and are high in iron, manganese, and magnesium. Regularly eating pepitas can fight anemia, increase fertility in men, and help to reduce cholesterol.

Crushed red pepper: Crushed red peppers, dried and crushed red chili peppers. They are spicy, but not as pungent as cayenne (which is ground red chili peppers). Crushed red pepper is a great source of capsaicin. Studies have shown that capsaicin is a natural pain reliever, fights cancer, revs the metabolism, and can relieve allergies. When used in the proper proportions, even babies can enjoy the health benefits of crushed red pepper. Both of my girls enjoy many dishes that include this ingredient.

Fresh ground black pepper: Some sort of peppercorn seems to be in just about every recipe in almost every type of cuisine. Why? It turns out that this is one super-healing berry. Yes, berry! Peppercorns are dried berries from the pepper plant. They are full of antioxidants, can help reduce gas, promote proper digestion, promote sweating (which helps rid the body of dangerous toxins), and are a natural diuretic. In ancient Greece, peppercorns were so valued that they were once used as a form of currency! It is best to grind your own pepper as needed to preserve the flavor and nutrients. Ground pepper loses its pungency in just a few months, so try to buy a three month supply at a time.

White pepper: White pepper is a milder version of the traditional black pepper. I use white pepper for lighter dishes, or when black speckles would make the dish less attractive. It is also a traditional ingredient in many Asian dishes. As far as health benefits, white pepper can help regulate the digestive tract, and is a natural anti-bacterial agent.

Pine nuts: I have to admit, before doing the research for this book, I never really thought about where pine nuts came from. It turns out, they come from pine trees (makes sense)! There are many different species of pine trees, but only about 20 of them can produce seeds large enough to harvest. Pine nuts are high in antioxidants (fight dangerous free radicals), vitamin E (helps wounds heal), and niacin (lowers cholesterol). I like to use them in small amounts as a garnish. Recently, pine nuts have been gaining popularity throughout the world. Their price has increased, but the flavor they add to a dish really is worth the money.

Crushed pineapple: Okay, we all know how great pineapple tastes. Now it's time to talk about how great it is for you. Pineapple is an amazing source of manganese (important for a healthy metabolism), bromelein (fights off inflammation), and vitamin C (promotes a healthy immune system). Some research suggests that the bromelein in pineapple can reduce the symptoms of inflammatory diseases such as rheumatoid arthritis, asthma, irritable bowel syndrome, and even acne! Crushed pineapple is a great way to add a natural sweetness to marinades and sauces. You can either buy it canned in its own juice (not in syrup), or make your own using a mini food processor.

Organic polenta: Polenta is corn that has been dried and coarsely ground. It is basically the whole grain version of grits. It can be served cake style, or as a base for Italian and European cuisine. Polenta can help prevent birth defects (folic acid), boost your memory (niacin), and reduce your risk of cancer (phytonutrients). Carbs are not the enemy.

Pork tenderloin: I have a good friend who is against eating pork. Because of that, I've done a ton of research on pigs. My conclusion is similar to my views on food in general. If you buy the standard factory farmed pork that is offered at most large supermarkets, you are most likely eating pork from pigs that were regularly given antibiotics, and raised in dirty, inhumane dwellings. These antibiotics are now going into your body, and possibly making you resistant to medicinal antibiotics when you really need them. Research also suggests that consuming meat poisoned with hormones and antibiotics is a contributing factor to the obesity problem in America. As with any meat, you need to look at quality. When purchasing pork, look for ones raised without antibiotics. If you have access to a local farmer, buy pastured pork. Pastured pork tastes amazing, and you can ask the farmer personally how she raised her pigs. I wish there was a cheap trick to get high quality animal protein, but there is not. All natural pork tenderloin is a great source of lean protein, and is rich in niacin, potassium, zinc, vitamin B6, and vitamin B12. I love it because it is quick cooking, tender, and is a nice change from chicken.

Baking potatoes: Ever since the Atkins craze, potatoes have gotten a horrible reputation. They are actually full of nutrients, and can be a great addition to any diet. The trick is to keep the skins, and to go light on the butter and cream (or leave it out altogether). Potatoes are rich in vitamin C, copper, manganese, vitamin B6, and fiber. Studies suggest that regularly eating potatoes can lower blood pressure, increase brain function, and help fuel your workouts.

Red potatoes: Did you know? Ounce for ounce, red potatoes have more potassium than bananas or spinach. The thin skin of red potatoes make them great for serving smashed, diced, or boiled. Red potatoes contain almost 60 different phytonutrients, can help lower blood pressure, and can help improve your memory.

Russet potatoes: see "Baking potatoes"

Sweet potatoes: Sweet potatoes have recently elevated to "superfood" status. This is because they are full of healing nutrients. Sweet potatoes can help stabilize blood sugar, protect against heart attack and stroke, and keep skin looking young and supple. When baked and pureed, sweet potatoes make a perfect baby food.

Proscuitto: Proscuitto is ham that has been cured (salted and air dried). It has a great flavor, and can even be eaten uncooked. Proscuitto is high in sodium, so go easy on the salt when cooking with it! If proscuitto is unavailable, feel free to substitute bacon (adjusting cooking times as necessary). Proscuitto contains iron to fight anemia, B vitamins to give you energy, and protein to help build muscle.

Roasted pumpkin: Once you realize how easy and tasty it is to roast your own pumpkin, you will probably be hooked! If you are too busy and decide to just buy a can of pumpkin instead, that is fine as well. The nutrients are super stars either way. Pumpkins are low in calories and packed with beta carotene, potassium, and fiber. Eating pumpkin will help fight the signs of anti-aging, reduce inflammation throughout the body, and fight the cells that can cause cancer.

Q

Queso fresco: Queso fresco is a crumbly white cheese popular in Spanish cuisine. Unlike most cheeses, queso fresco does not melt when heated, so it can turn a simple dinner into something very pretty. The translation of queso fresco is literally "fresh cheese". Therefore, pregnant mamas need to remember to source brands made from milk that has been pasteurized.

Quinoa: Quinoa (KEEN-wa) is an ancient "grain" that has recently been rediscovered, and is now considered by many as one of the top "superfoods". After doing further research, I discovered that quinoa is actually not a grain at all. It is technically an edible seed, and is a member of the chenopod family (the same one as spinach). In ancient times, the Incas fed quinoa to their soldiers before battle to give them the added stamina they needed to defeat their enemies. Quinoa is a complete protein, high in fiber, naturally gluten free, and full of phytonutrients and antioxidants.

R

Radishes: Radishes are an amazing way to detoxify the body. Studies have shown that eating radishes can help purify the blood, clean out the liver and kidneys, and fight off infection. It is also believed that eating radishes promotes healthy, vibrant skin. They contain folic acid, potassium, vitamin C, and copper. If you buy your radishes at the farmer's market, be sure to chop the greens off when you get home. (They are also edible.) The greens will leach moisture out of the radish, causing them to age quicker.

Golden raisins: Golden raisins are raisins made from green grapes. When sourcing organic "golden" raisins, you will notice that they are much darker than the blonde ones that are produced commercially. Commercially produced golden raisins are treated with sulfur dioxide and dried in heated ovens, not from the sun. Sulfur dioxide is a bleaching agent that prevents mold and is dangerous to your health. According to my research, sulfur dioxide is made from the oil of gasoline. (Yup.) It contains heavy metals, and can cause respiratory problems. It is also present in some brands of dried apricots and other dried fruits. Go organic!

Raisins: We all know what raisins are, right? Raisins are just dried grapes. If you have kiddos, I bet that these little gems are almost always sitting in your pantry. Using raisins is a great way to add natural sweetness to a dish. Just a small handful can completely eliminate the need for added sugar. Eating raisins can help maintain good eyesight, and are a great source of resveratrol and antioxidants. Grapes are often treated with pesticides, so please source organic whenever possible.

Brown basmati rice: Brown basmati rice is a tall and thin type of rice that stays much drier that the short grain varieties. It has a delicate aroma and, because it is not sticky, is great for stirring into soups, stews, and gumbos. Brown basmati rice is naturally gluten-free and full of fiber, B vitamins, and magnesium.

Brown jasmine rice: Jasmine rice is an aromatic rice with a nutty flavor that pairs beautifully with Thai and Asian dishes. When combined with chicken broth and a pinch of saffron, your taste buds will rejoice! Brown jasmine rice has all of the same benefits of brown rice. It is a good source of magnesium, selenium, and manganese.

Organic cooked brown rice, short grain: Did you know that rice grows in water? I guess I had never really given it much thought. I prefer the short grain variety of brown rice because it offers a chewier, nuttier flavor. I replace almost all processed white rice with it. I make an entire bag at a time, cook it in chicken broth, and then freeze it in one cup increments that I can defrost overnight in the fridge, or in just minutes using the microwave. Organic rice is only slightly more expensive than conventional, and you will be confident that it has not been sprayed with pesticides. Picking brown rice over white gives you more fiber, manganese, and B vitamins. Plus, it tastes better.

Wild rice: Wild rice has a great nutty, chewy texture that I absolutely adore! Wild rice has to be harvested by hand. This is the reason that it is more expensive than brown rice. It is technically not even a grain, but a grass, and full of healing nutrients. Wild rice is a good source of vegetarian protein, vitamin E, and folate.

Ricotta cheese: Did you know that leftover ricotta can be frozen for future use? It's true! Allow it to defrost in the refrigerator overnight and then proceed as written. Ricotta is a fresh whey cheese that originated in Italy. The English translation of ricotta is "cook again". That's because it is almost always cooked again (like in lasagna or cannoli). Ricotta is lower in fat than most cheese and a great way to add healthy protein to baked pasta dishes. Because it is very mild in flavor, it is also a great early protein source for babies.

Rockfish, wild caught: First off, I'm not really sure what rockfish is. I bought it at the Venice Whole Foods Market because it looked fresh, was on sale, had a cool name, and the fishmonger told me it would taste great steamed with ginger. Worked for me! When I started researching rockfish, I got very confused. I realized that some people call it Pacific snapper, some call it striped bass, and some say it can refer to upwards of 100 different types of fish. When using white fish, don't let the species of fish be your biggest concern. Buy what is fresh, sustainably raised, and in your price range. Tell your fishmonger whether you prefer a flaky or firm fish, and he can help guide you. Remember, fresh fish should never smell fishy and its skin should bounce back like a sponge. I often buy my fish frozen if I'm not going to use it on the day of purchase. Read the signs next time you are at the store. Many of the "fresh" fish in the display case have actually been "previously frozen". If you are just going to take it home and freeze it, you are paying extra money for the market to defrost a fish that you actually want frozen. That just seems silly.

Romaine lettuce: When it comes to crunchy lettuce, romaine tops the charts. Just two cups provides almost 150% of the current RDA for vitamin K! Vitamin K is crucial for building strong bones, helps support normal blood sugar levels, and promotes a healthy heart. Romaine lettuce also contains very good amounts of vitamins A and C, folate, manganese, potassium, copper, and fiber. Wow! The best part is you get all of this for less than 20 calories! Is your little one anti-lettuce? So is mine. I offer her the crunchy stems with the other salad components, and watch her pick around them every time. I'm not worried. She regularly sees us eating it, understands that it is healthy, and realizes it is something that her dad and I enjoy. Sooner or later, she will come around! By the way, iceberg lettuce is seriously lacking in nutrients compared to romaine. Make the switch!

Dried rosemary: I don't think I could make pizza sauce without dried rosemary. It harmonizes brilliantly with tomatoes. In dishes that have a longer cooking time or are baked at a higher heat, dried herbs are a shelf-stable, more affordable alternative to fresh. Luckily, most of the nutrients stay intact during the drying process. The only thing lost during the drying process is some of the volatile oils. Some brands add chemical preservatives to dried herbs. Source organic or buy from a trusted source to avoid this danger. To substitute dried herbs for fresh, replace 1 tsp of dried herbs for 1 tbsp of fresh herbs. Also, be sure to add the dried herbs earlier in the dish. It takes a while for the dried herbs to release their flavor.

Fresh rosemary: Rosemary is a type of evergreen shrub. It has a great pine smell and flavor, and is full of health benefits. Rosemary promotes good digestion, is a natural immunity booster, reduces the severity of asthma, and can improve cognitive skills. It is a staple in savory European cooking, and adds a cozy aroma to your whole home.

S

Saffron threads: I will tell you up front that saffron threads are not cheap. If you live near a Trader Joe's, buy them there. They offer great quality at a great price. If not, take the plunge. Saffron adds a great delicate flavor to rice, light sauces, and soups. It is also has incredible medicinal benefits. Saffron is considered an aphrodisiac, can help lower bad cholesterol, fights cancer, can improve asthma and arthritis, improves memory, and boosts the immune system.

Fresh sage: Did you know that the Latin word for sage (salvere) translates, "to be saved"? That's a pretty big claim for a little herb! In centuries past, the Arabs believed sage promoted immortality, Europeans believed it protected them from witchcraft, and the Romans held a special ceremony when it was time to gather it. In modern times, studies have shown that the flavonoids, phenolic acids, and rosemarinic acids in sage can help reduce inflammation in the body, lessen the severity of asthma, stabilize the GI tract, promote a healthy metabolism, boost your cognitive skills, and slow the progression of Alzheimer's disease. Plus it adds a great savory flavor to soups, stews, appetizers, tomato sauces, and potatoes. The leaves also taste great crisped up in the oven.

Wild salmon: Wild salmon is one of the things that I am passionate about. I will not eat farm raised Atlantic salmon. Farm raised salmon are fed animal by-products (not fit for human consumption), high amounts of antibiotics (to fight off the disease and sea lice these fish acquire from being kept pent up in small, netted areas), and chemicals to give them their orange color. That's right, most farmed salmon are so depleted in nutrients and omega-3 that they are injected with chemical dyes. Their actual color is a mealy grey, but the companies that sell these fish assume that consumers would have no interest in purchasing grey salmon. So, they make it even unhealthier by adding chemicals to the antibiotic, genetically modified fed fish. I would eat conventional beef and poultry before farmed salmon. It is disgusting. However, regularly eating wild salmon supports a healthy heart, cardiovascular system, and immune system. The omega-3 essential fatty acids help you maintain a healthy weight and are a natural anti-inflammatory. Wild salmon feast on omega-3 rich krill. This is where they get their beautiful orange color. The more colorful the fillet, the more omega-3 it contains. If you cannot afford wild salmon (preferably Alaskan), I would suggest that you avoid eating salmon altogether. (Wow, that was harsh!)

Jarred salsa: I admit it. I love jarred salsa. (More specifically, I love the fresh, jarred salsa from our favorite local Mexican restaurant.) Obviously, you want to avoid high fructose corn syrup and/or hydrogenated oils, but I've rarely seen those ingredients listed. Prepared salsa is a great helper in the kitchen. I use it in salad dressing, with quesadillas, burritos, whatever. It tastes great stirred into soups, or as a layer in dips. Eating salsa with organic tortilla chips will help your body absorb some of the fat-soluble nutrients it contains (like you needed an excuse). Salsa is low in calories and rich in health benefits. Feasting on salsa can boost your metabolism and immunity, keep your blood pressure at an optimal level, and is a natural anti-bacterial agent.

Salsa Verde: Salsa Verde is a green salsa made with simple ingredients such as tomatillos, jalapeño, cilantro, and lime. I have enjoyed many mild brands that are made using only whole, pronounceable ingredients. (Many grocers make it in-house.) However, food manufactures can be sneaky. Please double check the ingredient list and source an alternative brand if you see the following chemically laden terms: high fructose corn syrup, monosodium glutamate (MSG), or hydrogenated oils. Also, notice whether the jar is labeled "mild", "medium", or "hot". Be sure to source a mild variety if serving to children or guests with tender palates. Tomatillos are low in calories, but high in potassium, niacin, and vitamin C.

Sea salt: I choose sea salt for all of my cooking for two reasons. As a foodie, it tastes better. Sea salt is less refined, more flavorful, and coarser. Therefore, as a healthnut, I am satisfied using less sea salt than I would table salt. Because it is less refined, it also contains more trace minerals than table salt. Keep in mind that the majority of salt in the typical American diet comes from processed, prepackaged foods. By eliminating these from your diet, you will enjoy a healthier, more energized life.

Sweet Italian sausage: Regardless of whether it is made using chicken, turkey, or pork, I love Italian sausage. The combination of fennel seeds, Romano cheese, parsley, and garlic just make meat taste great! Always remember to source sausage made from animals raised without added hormones or antibiotics. I have found a local farmer that actually makes her own. It is tasty!

Scallions: see green onions

Sea scallops: Once I realized that I could prepare restaurant quality scallops in my own kitchen in less than 10 minutes, I was hooked! Scallops are a great source of vitamin B12 (which many Americans are deficient in) and heart healthy omega-3's. Thanks to the high amount of magnesium in scallops, they are also helpful in preventing metabolic syndrome, improving cognitive function, and building bone density.

Seasoned salt: Seasoned salt is salt seasoned with a large variety of herbs and spices. I like to use it in recipes where a light seasoning is needed, but I don't want to measure 1/16 or 1/24 teaspoon of 12 different spices (as if). Even the common Lawry's brand is MSG free, but you will want to double check the brand you are purchasing just to make sure. Researchers have concluded that consuming MSG (monosodium glutamate) can trigger migraines, chest pain, numbness, and muscle weakness. Children and those with compromised immune systems are even more susceptible to its effects. It has become a fairly easy ingredient to avoid, so I do.

Sesame oil: Sesame oil is a staple in Asian cooking. I prefer to buy toasted sesame oil from an Asian market. If there is no Asian market in your area, look in the Asian section of your local grocer for brands made in Japan. Sesame oil is made from sesame seeds and contains omega 3, 6, and 9. Omega essential fatty acids are able to prevent and slow the progression of chronic disease. The lingams in sesame oil can help lower blood pressure. Sesame oil also contains phytonutrients and high levels of vitamin E. Plus, it makes a dish taste so good!

Sesame seeds: Sesame seeds are a good source of many minerals including copper, manganese, tryptophan, calcium, magnesium, iron, and zinc. Regularly consuming sesame seeds can reduce the symptoms of rheumatoid arthritis, help lower cholesterol and blood pressure, prevent migraines, and promote a healthy liver. They also taste great and add a crunchy, nutty flavor to many dishes!

Dry sherry: Using dry sherry in cooking is a great way to add a rich and savory flavor to a dish. Sherry is also a suitable stand-in for rice wine in Asian cooking. I feel completely comfortable serving the foods I prepare with sherry to my kids. I use the smallest amount possible, and I know that between 50% and 95% of the alcohol evaporates during the cooking process. Divide that by the amount of food that they actually consume, and the amount of alcohol is practically immeasurable. If you do not feel comfortable cooking with sherry, you may substitute chicken, vegetable, or beef broth.

Shrimp: Shrimp are an amazing source of vitamins D and B12. Both of these are vitamins in which many Americans are deficient. Shrimp are also lower in mercury than almost any other seafood. They are a great source of lean protein, selenium, and tryptophan. They can help protect from heart disease, improve the cardiovascular system, and help prevent Alzheimer's. I love the fact that they can be prepared in just three minutes! When you purchase shrimp, please look for Pacific white shrimp grown in the USA. This will help boost our economy, and lower the amount of fuel needed to import farm raised fish from other countries.

Soba noodles: Soba noodles are a traditional Japanese noodle made out of buckwheat flour. Buckwheat is a whole grain that is also gluten-free. This makes soba noodles an ideal choice for those sensitive to gluten. Some brands do mix wheat flour with buckwheat flour, so always read labels. Buckwheat (which is technically a fruit seed) can help stabilize blood sugar levels, lower cholesterol, and eliminate toxins from the liver.

Sour cream: I have to tell you (again), I love sour cream. It adds a tanginess and creaminess to many dishes at about 1/3 of the fat and calories found in equal amounts of butter, cream, or mayonnaise. Sour cream is a cultured product, but not fully fermented. It must be kept refrigerated and should be discarded when mold develops. Sour cream contains calcium, vitamin K, healthy bacteria, potassium, and phosphorus. I admit, I mostly like it for the flavor.

Light soy sauce: Soy sauce is another staple in Asian cooking. It adds a complexity of flavors that cannot be otherwise replicated. I prefer to buy organic "shout" (Japanese for soy sauce) that has been made in Japan. This ensures that my soy sauce is made in an authentic style, and without the use of genetically modified soy, chemical fertilizers, or dangerous pesticides. A little goes a long way, so a high quality brand is worth the investment. As a healthnut, I recognize that soy sauce contains a high amount of sodium. When creating recipes, I try to use the minimum amount of soy sauce possible without compromising the quality of the finished product.

Mushroom flavored dark soy sauce: When my amazingly talented friend Fenche taught me how to create stir-fries and fried rice, she said, "You have to finish it with this sauce. It is the only way to get the rich, deep color and flavor." She was so adamant about its greatness that she gave me a bottle as my going away present when I left Los Angeles. (She didn't think it could be found it in Kansas, but it can). It is made in China and adds the essence of mushroom to a traditional soy sauce. It also has a thicker consistency. To keep the desired texture and flavor, this sauce should be added at the completion of a dish, even after the heat has been removed. Season to taste, and enjoy truly authentic Chinese flavor! As of July 13, 2010, and according to greenpeace.org, both Pearl River Bridge (my favorite), and Lee Kum Kee are GMO-free. Please verify as ingredients are always changing.

Reduced sodium soy sauce: If you are watching your sodium intake, this is the soy sauce for you. It contains 25% - 45% less sodium than traditional soy sauce (depending on brands). I also like to use this in dishes where the saltiness of regular soy sauce would be overpowering. Be sure to source organic or non-GMO varieties to avoid genetically modified soy; which has caused high levels of infertility in animal studies.

Frozen organic spinach: Frozen organic spinach is one of my favorite convenience and budget foods. One 16-ounce package of frozen spinach contains the equivalent to over two pounds of fresh, all for about the cost of one 5-ounce bag! Now that's a deal. It becomes an even bigger deal when you read the health benefits of spinach directly below.

Organic spinach: Spinach is consistently on EWG's dirty dozen list. If available, I always buy it organically. Regardless, spinach contains more nutrients per calorie than almost any other green food. It contains tons of bone building vitamin K, as well as substantial amounts of vitamins A, C, and B2. Additionally, spinach is rich in manganese, potassium, magnesium, calcium, and iron. When used to finish a dish, it easily wilts. This makes it simple to feed your family 5 cups of fresh, nutrient dense spinach in a single meal!

Sirloin steak: Sirloin is a lean cut of beef that, in my opinion, does not have much flavor. However, it is inexpensive, and when properly marinated and prepared, it takes on whatever flavor profile you ask of it. I use sirloin in stir-fries and other Asian dishes often! When I see a sale on grass-fed sirloin, I stock my freezer. Healthy beef is a fabulous source of CLA (conjugated linoleic acid), which is a great way to help prevent cancer. It is also rich in iron, zinc, and vitamin B12.

Organic sugar: I do not use white sugar in my cooking and baking. Period. I believe that it is a worthless, disease-causing product. In moderation, I do like organic sugar, and enjoy adding a pinch to vinaigrettes, curries, and other dishes that need just a boost. Organic sugar is also sweeter than refined sugar, making it possible to cut calories overall. Organic sugar contains potassium, magnesium, iron, and calcium. Refined sugar is void of all nutrients. Refined sugar is also treated with dangerous chemicals during the bleaching process. You really should upgrade!

T

Dried tarragon: I love dried tarragon. It adds a great flavor to a variety of dishes. I find that a little goes a long way, making it a great, cost effective ingredient. Most of the nutrients stay intact during the drying process. The only thing lost is some of the volatile oils. Some brands add chemical preservatives to dried herbs, so please source organic or buy from a trusted source to avoid this danger. To substitute dried herbs for fresh, replace 1 tsp of dried herbs for 1 tbsp of fresh herbs. Also, be sure to add the dried herbs earlier in the dish. It takes a while for the dried herbs to release their flavor.

Fresh tarragon: Did you know tarragon is actually a member of the sunflower family? Interesting. Tarragon can help fight fatigue, aid in digestion, and reduce blood pressure. It also tastes really yummy!

Dried thyme: Dried herbs are a shelf-stable, more affordable alternative to fresh. Luckily, most of the nutrients stay intact during the drying process. The only thing lost during the drying process is some of the volatile oils. Some brands add chemical preservatives to dried herbs, please source organic or buy from a trusted source to avoid this danger. To substitute dried herbs for fresh, replace 1 tsp of dried herbs for 1 tbsp of fresh herbs. Also, be sure to add the dried herbs earlier in the dish. It takes a while for the dried herbs to release their flavor.

Fresh thyme: I love thyme! (I know.) For awhile, I thought thyme was one of those things that just enhanced fall and winter dishes. It does, but it also works year-round. After growing thyme for the first thyme (sorry) this past summer, I realized that this was a year round goodie. Thyme naturally has anti-bacterial properties, boosts the immune system, and promotes cardiovascular health. The fresh leaves of thyme can take a mixed green salad to the next level (thyme-lemon vinaigrette), and the fact that it can aid in a natural weight loss program makes it awesome!

Tomato sauce: Simply prepared tomato sauce is a great way to add moisture and flavor to a variety of dishes without adding extra salt or fat. If available, try to buy from brands that use BPA-free liners or are packaged using the tetra-pak (cardboard box type of thing). If you are a total rock star and take the time to make your own, 1¾ cup equals the amount in a 15-ounce can. Tomato sauce is, cooked and pureed tomatoes. It is an excellent source of lycopene, vitamin C, and can help lower cholesterol.

Beefsteak tomatoes: Tomatoes are one of the current rock stars in the produce world. Packed with lycopene, phytonutrients, vitamin C, and fiber, these should be a daily staple. Regularly consuming tomatoes can help stabilize blood sugar, and offers protection against many types of cancer.

Cherry/grape tomatoes: I love these little gems for the way they add color, flavor, and nutrients to almost any dish. Tomatoes can help reduce your risk of heart disease, lower LDL (bad) cholesterol, and help your body properly metabolize food. Plus, they taste amazing and are available year round.

Crushed tomatoes: I dream of one day growing and harvesting an abundance of tomatoes. Until then, I am thankful for the BPA-free brands that do it for me. Crushed tomatoes make an amazing sauce for pizza, thicken up a Bolognese, and enhance a variety of Italian based recipes. Crushed tomatoes have to be heated before canning. This makes them higher in cancer preventing and natural detoxifying lycopene than tomatoes that are eaten raw.

Heirloom tomatoes: Heirloom tomatoes are tomatoes in their purest form. They are the way unadulterated tomatoes have naturally evolved in response to pests and climate, and far superior in flavor and nutrients when compared to supermarket tomatoes. Also called "ugly tomatoes", heirloom tomatoes come in beautiful purples, greens, yellows, oranges, and reds. If you have access to heirlooms, please take advantage of them!

Peeled tomatoes: Whole peeled tomatoes are tomatoes that have been blanched and then had the skin removed. They are packed in their juices and are a cost effective way to enjoy large quantities of tomatoes year round. When possible, I always purchase organic canned goods. This way I know that they have not been preserved with dangerous chemicals.

Plum tomatoes: I like plum tomatoes because they are available nationwide year round. They are also lower in water content than beefier tomatoes. This makes them a suitable stand-in for canned and drained tomatoes. Cooking plum tomatoes raises the level of lycopene. Lycopene helps to reduce the progression of chronic disease, asthma, and heart problems. Lycopene is fat-soluble so it is important to always enjoy tomatoes with a bit of yummy, fresh mozzarella or extra virgin olive oil.

Organic corn tortilla chips: Organic corn tortilla chips are a staple in our house. We eat them with salsa, guacamole, bean dip, taco salads, as a "breading" for southwestern chicken, the list goes on! I always purchase organic ones to ensure that I am protecting my family from the dangers of genetically modified corn or hydrogenated oils. When eaten in moderation, tortilla chips can absolutely be part of a healthy diet.

Organic corn tortillas: Purchasing organic corn tortillas will help protect your family from the genetically modified corn and hydrogenated oils that are commonly used in the conventional brands. Corn is a good source of niacin (which helps build good cholesterol), folate (which helps prevent birth defects), and phosphorus (which aids in proper digestion).

Whole wheat tortillas: Whole wheat tortillas have come a long way. Unfortunately, many are still laden with high fructose corn syrup and partially hydrogenated oils. Please read labels carefully. An ideal whole wheat tortilla should contain whole wheat, olive oil, filtered water, and salt (and maybe a pinch of sugar). Regularly consuming whole wheat products can help you keep from developing metabolic syndrome, help you to maintain a healthy weight, and keep your bowel functions regular.

Canned chunk light tuna packed in water: Seafood is still considered healthy, some varieties more than others. My favorite varieties of wild caught fish are often out of my price range. I am thankful for light chunk tuna packed in water for days that I just cannot justify the cost of my adored halibut or wild salmon. When you limit your consumption of canned tuna to just two cans a week, it can provide many health benefits without significantly raising your risk of mercury poisoning. Just four ounces of tuna provides your body with large amounts of tryptophan (which can help reduce anxiety) and selenium (which helps fight cancer cells and promotes a healthy immune system). It is also an amazing source of lean protein, a great way to help build lean muscle tone, and aid in weight loss.

Turmeric: Turmeric is what makes mustard yellow. It's true! It is also full of amazing, healthful nutrients. Turmeric is one of the strongest anti-inflammatories around. Studies have shown that turmeric offers relief from rheumatoid arthritis, irritable bowel syndrome, and cystic fibrosis.

U

Dried udon noodles: Udon noodles are a Japanese wheat noodle. The Japanese have conducted studies that show udon noodles are digested very quickly and without spiking blood sugar. They also believe that udon noodles can help fight symptoms of the flu (kind of like our chicken soup). Udon noodles contain thiamine (which aids in digestion), niacin (which can help lower cholesterol and aids in detoxification), and zinc (which aids in reproduction and memory). I love udon noodles chewy texture, high protein content (for a noodle), and the fact that I can use them to create a toddler friendly meal in minutes!

V

Apple cider vinegar: I drink a diluted tablespoon of apple cider vinegar almost every morning. There are entire books written about its health benefits! Regularly consuming apple cider vinegar can help you maintain a healthy weight, reduce plaque buildup, fight infection, and stabilize blood sugar. (To find out more, Google it!) My theory is that if vinegar can clean and sanitize my house, it can help clean and sanitize my body as well.

Balsamic vinegar: Once upon a time, I used plain balsamic vinegar to dress my salads. Since then, I've learned that healthy oils are just as important as low calorie vinegars for absorbing nutrients. I will say that the sweet, thick texture of balsamic vinegar was always immensely satisfying. Balsamic vinegar is made from pressing sweet trebbiano grapes and then allowing them to ferment in oak barrels. Balsamic vinegar promotes a healthy digestive tract, helps stabilize blood sugar, and boosts the flavor of greens and berries with a negligible amount of calories.

Red wine vinegar: Vinegar has been used medicinally for many, many centuries. While not as famous as apple cider vinegar, regular consumption of red wine vinegar has been shown to help lower high triglyceride levels and blood pressure. It helps remove plaque from the heart, and is a great way to add fat and calorie-free flavor to any dish.

Rice vinegar: Rice vinegar (not to be confused with *seasoned* rice vinegar) is made simply from fermented wine. It is a mild vinegar that is popular in Asian cooking. Rice vinegar has strong antiseptic powers. Some speculate that rice vinegar was originally added to sushi rice to kill any bacteria that may be lingering in the raw fish. As a healthnut and a foodie, rice vinegar is a great way to add flavor to a variety of dishes with zero fat and minimal calories.

White wine vinegar: White wine vinegar is a great way to boost your body's ability to absorb the calcium and other minerals found in salad greens. Vinegar fights infection, helps reduce inflammation, and can help detoxify the body.

W

Wagon wheel shaped noodles: I've loved wagon wheel shaped noodles for as long as I can remember. Something about their fun shape makes me happy. Unfortunately, they are becoming harder and harder to find. If wagon wheels are not available in your market, substitute fusilli (cork screw) or farfalle (bow-tie) noodles. (You can also buy them online.) As far as the health benefits, please see "organic pasta".

Candied walnuts: Walnuts are one of the top sources for omega-3 fatty acids. When candied with organic sugar and butter or olive oil, they can take a salad to whole new levels. I love them with any basic vinaigrette, mixed greens, fresh berries, and whatever else I have on hand. Regularly consuming walnuts promotes a healthy heart, a healthy cardiovascular system, a healthy immune system, and helps fight the side effects of eczema! Please avoid walnuts that have been candied in corn syrup and/or vegetable oil. Those can negate the benefits of the healthful nuts.

Walnuts: Walnuts are a tasty way to add flavor and nutrients to a variety of meals. They can help prevent thickening of the arteries, stabilize blood sugar, and lower cholesterol. They are often considered a brain food, both because of their brain-like appearance, and because of their high amounts of cognitive boosting omega-3 fatty acids. Snack on walnuts before your next test or presentation, it may just give you the boost you need!

Walnut oil: One of our favorite snacks is fresh whole wheat bread dipped in high quality walnut oil. It is super yummy and a treat I can feel good about sharing with my girls. One serving of walnut oil contains almost 100% of your RDA for omega-3s. It also has manganese, helps reduce the symptoms of eczema, and boosts your cognitive abilities (makes you smart). The healthy fat in walnut oil will help you feel satiated after consuming just a small amount. As a foodie, it just tastes awesome!

Water chestnuts: Water chestnuts are sweet and crunchy root vegetables that grow in water. Popular in Asian cuisine, I love to throw them into a dish that is missing the crunch factor. They are one of the few ingredients I still buy in a can. (The fresh ones are hard to come by in most markets.) If you do run across the fresh, take advantage! According to eastern medicine, eating water chestnuts is a good way to naturally detoxify the body, relieve bloating, and they are a natural diuretic.

Red wine: Red wine can be healing in small amounts, but detrimental in large amounts. Red wine contains resveratrol. Studies have shown resveratrol can help lower cholesterol and prevent heart disease. Red wine also has high levels of antioxidants. Antioxidants help fight cancer, boost the immune system, and help reduce inflammation throughout the body. If your family chooses not to use red wine in cooking, feel free to substitute a mixture of grape juice and red wine vinegar in its place. For 1 cup of red wine, substitute ½ cup Concord grape juice, 2 tablespoons red wine vinegar, and ⅓ cup water. It will slightly change the flavor profile of a dish, but does make a suitable substitution.

White wine: A small amount of white wine adds a great flavor to many savory dishes while contributing a minimal amount of fat and calories. I feel confident serving my girls any of the dishes in which I use wine. Studies have shown that 50% to 95% of the alcohol in wine is evaporated during cooking. When you combine that with the actual portion size that a child is eating, it is not something that I am worried about. If you would rather not use wine in cooking, use this easy substitute. For ¼ cup of white wine, substitute 3 tbsp chicken broth and 1 tbsp lemon juice.

Worcestershire sauce: A splash of Worcestershire sauce is a great way to give meat dishes the "je ne sais quoi" factor. A mixture of vinegar, molasses, anchovies, tamarind, and a host of other flavorings, Worcestershire sauce is definitely hard to describe. When purchasing, be sure to read the labels. Some brands try to sneak high fructose corn syrup into the mix! (At the time of printing, French's and Annie's natural brands of Worcestershire sauce were both high fructose corn syrup free.)

X

Y

Z

Resources:

In the Internet age, it would be impossible to source every single website and/or blog that has assisted me in becoming the healthnut foodie that I am today. The information that I've shared in this book comes from over a decade of research and personal discovery. The websites listed below are the trusted resources that I return to again and again. If my book leaves you thirsty for more, please give these sites a peek. They contain a wealth of information and knowledge.

http://www.healthnutfoodie.com

http://www.healthychild.org

http://www.whfoods.org

http://www.ewg.org

http://www.greenpeace.org

http://www.organicconsumers.org

http://www.drgreene.com

http://www.wisegeek.com

http://www.drmercola.com

http://www.wikipedia.com

http://www.sixwise.com

Acknowledgements:

To the Creator of the universe, thank you for giving us everything we would need to excite the palate, heal the body, and nourish the soul when You created the earth.

To my amazing husband, Darren, thank you for being my rock and my soul mate. I cannot imagine doing life with anyone else. Thank you for your patience, your love, your support, and for turning me into the foodie that I am today. I am no longer afraid of butter.

To my amazing parents, thank you for never telling me that my dreams were too big. Thank you for showing me unconditional love and for turning our family's dinner table into a place of acceptance, life lessons, and joy. To my sister, Betsy, you are my fellow dreamer and the girl that knows me inside out and backwards. I am so thankful that my little girls will get to experience the same special friendship that we do. Thank you also for taking the amazing photo that graces the cover of this book. It totally rocks!

Rachel Jenks, thank you for your generous friendship and designing such an amazing cover. I thank God our paths collided. Christina Neil, thank you for being my copy editor, for your information on how to succeed in self-publishing, and for being a kindred spirit. You both radiate beauty from the inside out. Karey Jones, thank you for pushing me to the finish line, dishing out marketing advice, and offering me friendship. I look forward to raising our kids together. To my Los Angeles' M.I.L.K. mamas, I could not have gotten through the first two years of parenting without you. This cookbook was inspired by the conversations we had sitting on your living room floors. I dream of the day I can, once again, hug you in person. To the cynical Izzy Moon, thank you for being you and for asking the question that made me realize I needed to change the way Americans feed their families. ("What are you going to do when Annie gets invited to a friend's house for dinner? Tell her not to eat?" Smart aleck.)

To my Lord and Savior, Jesus Christ, thank You for giving me life, forgiving my many sins, and for enabling me to help You impact my one small corner of the world. The journey is just beginning!

Finally, to all of you that I have ever shared a conversation about food or health, thank you for contributing to my opinion on life and the way we should eat. One meal at a time, we will make a difference!

About the author...

Katie Newell is a reformed junk food junkie on a mission
to change the way we feed our families. After switching to a
real food way of eating, and by the grace of God, Katie
noticed relief from some of the debilitating effects of a chronic
and painful disease that has plagued her since childhood.
She was also able to triumph over infertility after being told
she had no hope. In an attempt to prevent today's children from
having to suffer the way she did, Katie has teamed up with her
chef husband, Darren, to create fresh, fast, and delicious
recipes that rival the food being served in popular upscale
restaurants. Katie and Darren are making it their mission to
teach today's children just how tasty real food can be.
Katie is also the founder of healthnutfoodie.com and has had
her work featured on dozens of websites, including cnn.com,
healthychild.org, and drgreene.com. The Newells believe that
good food is a gift that should be celebrated. They want to
share that gift, and the celebration, with you.